Tales of Old

Tales of
Old Derbyshire

~

Elizabeth Eisenberg

With Illustrations by Don Osmond

COUNTRYSIDE BOOKS
NEWBURY, BERKSHIRE

First published 1992
© Elizabeth Eisenberg 1992

COUNTRYSIDE BOOKS
3 CATHERINE ROAD
NEWBURY, BERKSHIRE

ISBN 1 85306 193 X

Produced through MRM Associates Ltd., Reading
Typeset by Paragon Typesetters, Queensferry
Printed in England by J. W. Arrowsmith Ltd., Bristol

To My Family

Contents

DERBYSHIRE – The map overleaf is by John Speede, and shows the county as it was in the early seventeenth century.

THE ARMES of all those Honorable Famylyes, as have borne the Dignitye and Title of Earles of Darbye, from the tyme of the Normans Conquest unto this present

William Ferres

Ed. E. of Lancastre

John of Gante D. of L.

Thomas Standley

PART OF CHESHIRE

HIGH PEAK HUND.

PART OF

DARBYE

STAFFORDSHIR

A Scale of pases

YORK SHIRE

Part

of

Notting

ham

Shire

Sheafeld
Healey Bridge
Wales
Harthill
The Shire okes
Beghton
Kilmarsh
Norton
Eckington
Barlebrugh
Whitwell
Dremfild
Clowns
Clownechurch
Cresswell
Welbeck
Helbck
SCARSDALE
Whittenton
Woodsbury
Ebeston
Chester
Whaley
Nether Langwith
feld
Scarby
Palterton
Hingham
Clapwell
Pleafly
HUND.
Hardwick
Hackney
Rowthorp
Maunisfild
Pilfly
Teversall
Nottinghall
Higham
Malurell
South Normanton
Carling thwat hall
Alfreton
Pynxon
Swanwick
Somercrouss
Ufton
Wingfild
Wansley
Brunsley
Crich
Cotton
Cabor
Ripley
Morley park
Heanor
Denbye
Langley
Shipls
WIRKESWORTH
Kelburn
Smaly
C. Cossall
Nelbrch
Heasley park
Morton underwood
Ilkeston
Trowell
Morley
Halam
Kirk
Halam
Stanton
MORLE
STON
Stanley
Staplesford
Kerr
Braesall
Attnten
Chaddsdon
Hopwell
Longeston
Darwent Sept
Ambaston
Sandi
Kisler
Little Wilne Swaley
Darbye
Lytharch
Brayston
Great Oure
Little Oure
Osmaston
Normanton
Thurlaston
Chelaston
Great Welne
Sherlow
Elwell
Syfsfild
Barrow
Swarston
Aston
Arleston
Finderon
Twysford
Willston
Swarb
Wetson
Stanli
Farmerton
Melborne
Newton
Melborne cast
Castle Donyngton
Melton
Tichnell

PART

OF

LECESTER

Harsham
Cookes
Stanton
REPPINGTON
Smalingwon
Slaughter
Knighton
Aubill
Castle Greasley
Oakly
Ashbye de la Zouche
Packington
HUND.
Over Seal
Nether Seal
Meshen
Normanton
Seale Greasly
Appleby
Chiloote
Swenne
Jodocus Hondius celavit

SHIRE

DIEV ET . ON DROIT

Anno
DARBIESHIRE
deſcribed
1 6 1 0

The Scale of Miles

Performed by John Speede, and are to be ſold in
popes head Alley by John Sudbury and G. Humble

Iodocus Hondius celavit

BUXTON

Sainte Annes well

A Cold Spring

The
Derbyshire Streakers

THERE'S nothing new about streaking in Derbyshire. A race run by naked boys used to take place every winter in villages situated in the north of the county. According to the natives, these annual competitions were handed down from the Greeks and no other county bred men strong enough to take part in them. There is certainly no record of similar races anywhere else in the world after the Greek Olympics were discontinued.

Two of these races were witnessed by a Mr. Forrest in 1755. Riding from Chesterfield to Worksop one cold winter's day, he was surprised, when he entered 'the township of Staverly' to find crowds gathering in the highways and lanes. On enquiring the reason, he was told that the naked boys' race was about to begin.

He forced his way through the throng to the starting point where he found four sturdy youths, aged about sixteen and all nearly six feet tall, stark naked and apparently quite unaffected by the icy ground and the keen northerly wind.

The three miles they had to run took the contestants round the village of Brimington and then back to Staveley. Many bets were made as the excitement mounted and the boys were reported to be running close together. In the end a boy called Flaxey Rotherham won by no more than one stride.

When Mr. Forrest heard that a similar race was to be run

in Whitwell the following day, he 'made haste to arrive at that village and laid overnight at the George Inn where the race was to start on the morrow'.

The length of this race was two miles and it was also run on a circular course round the village. The crowds were even bigger than at Staveley, onlookers coming from as far afield as Sheffield, Mansfield, Chesterfield and Derby.

At that time, reported Mr. Forrest, the population of Whitwell was no more than '700 souls' but, on this occasion, at least a thousand visitors added to the total. It had been freezing overnight but nobody paid attention to the weather, neither did the nakedness of the boys appear to embarrass the spectators, many of whom were women.

Six boys were taking part in the race. One of them turned out to be the previous day's winner who was a native of Whitwell and was first favourite in the betting. Among deafening cheers, Flaxey won by six strides and was immediately hoisted shoulder high by the other five competitors and carried round the village. 'I marvelled,' wrote Mr. Forrest 'that the lads were not stricken with mortal cold. Their bodies were steaming and not even a cloak was offered them until the end of the parade which lasted about an hour.

On their return to the inn, they were each supplied with a large mug of mulled ale, piping hot, and were then rubbed down with coarse sacking. After putting on their shirts and breeches, they sat down to a meal specially prepared for them. This consisted of two flat oatcakes spread with honey and topped with best Derbyshire cheese, followed by extra large portions of bull's beef. The steaks had been beaten with wooden mallets for an hour before being cooked in order to tenderise them and Mr. Forrest noted that 'the meat was very rare and the blood ran freely with the knife'. Finally, they were served with great helpings of apple pie and more mulled ale. By this time the whole company was 'singing and joking in a good humoured manner'.

In contrast to the Naked Boys' races in the arctic conditions of north east Derbyshire, annual races for girls and women (there was no age limit) were held in Derby and surrounding villages in the warmer weather of August. Although the females were allowed to wear one single garment, many of the competitors chose to run totally naked. In Derby, one of these contests took place on August 7th 1735. The contestants were six young women, described in a local newspaper report as 'not incommoded by either clothes or modesty' who ran three times round an area in Derby called Moorfield.

There was a large crowd of spectators, 'generous with their applause' and, apparently, no rivalry as to who should come first in the race for everyone who finished was presented with half a guinea and a new smock.

Races of this kind were abandoned during the 18th century after increasing pressure from the Church Authorities. The clergy condemned such exhibitions as 'barbarous and vulgar'.

The
Human Calculator

THE village of Elmton was called, in the Domesday Book, Helmetune meaning the farm in the elms. It lies between Bolsover and Creswell not far from the Nottingham border and forms a small oasis of agricultural land surrounded by mining villages.

The old parish church consisted of 'three Isles and one Cross Isle with a steeple and tower in the centre thereof'. Its registers dated from 1559. The old vicarage was situated in the corner of a field known as 'Vicar's Close' and, at the end of the 17th century, the vicar was the Reverend John Buxton whose son, William Buxton, was the village schoolmaster.

It was William's second child, Jedidiah, who has been called 'the most amazing calculator in history'. Born on March 20th 1707, Jedidiah caused his father and grandfather much concern when it became apparent after he started school that he was incapable of learning to read or write and was never able to sign his name. But he had an extraordinary passion for numbers and attained such a degree of skill in reckoning that he became the wonder of the neighbourhood. It was said that mental arithmetic occupied his mind to such an extent that his brain was unable to cope with anything else.

When fully grown, his mental age, discounting his powers of reckoning, was that of a child of ten and he spent all his working life as a farm labourer.

He never wrote down figures but made calculations in his head, memorising the answers to complicated sums and producing them months later. The villagers delighted in devising mathematical problems for him to solve such as working out the product of a farthing doubled 139 times. The answer to this, given in a very short time, was expressed in pounds stretching to 39 figures and Jedidiah then multiplied this sum by itself.

The local squire, Sir John Rodes of Barlborough Hall, invited Jedidiah to measure up the estate. After pacing out the fields and woods, he produced the total area in acres, roods and perches and then to amuse himself, converted the result into square inches. Checked by a surveyor, these figures were found to be correct.

During services in church he passed the time by counting the number of words in the hymns, prayers and psalms and, instead of paying attention to the proclamations of the sermon, he calculated how many words the vicar delivered per minute.

Jedidiah could say exactly how many pints of beer he had drunk since he was 12 years of age, calling a pint a 'wind' because he said it needed only one wind to swallow a pint.

It took 1½ minutes for him to find how many times a coach wheel of 6 ft diameter would revolve in travelling the 204 miles between London and York. In the same time he worked out how many barleycorns would reach 8 miles.

Any space of time he changed into minutes and converted distances into hairsbreadths. For large numbers he invented his own names like 'tribe' for the cube of a million and 'cramp' for a thousand tribe of tribes.

The most amazing aspect of Jedidiah's genius was that, while making these colossal calculations he was able to carry on a conversation and answer questions about other matters. He could also break off his reckoning, turn his attention to another subject and continue with the original calculation some time afterwards. In tackling a profound or lengthy problem, however, he became silent and appeared to be 'regardless of all external objects, undisturbed by any noise'. In his own words he was 'drunk wi' reckoning' and often needed a good sleep to recover from the strain.

At length, Jedidiah's phenomenal expertise with numbers came to the notice of the general public. In 1751 several people wrote about him to the *Gentleman's Magazine* demanding that 'this poor, obscure man should be rescued from oblivion'. Examples of his incredible calculations were given together with the statement that there had not been such a 'genius of mental reckoning since the days of the Roman Empire'. One article deplored the fact that 'this Derbyshire genius, clothed in rags, has to labour hard with his spade in order to support a large family' and begged the readers to supply some financial help.

There is no record of such assistance being forthcoming nor that Jedidiah had any children. It is known that he had a wife for her death was recorded in 1753 and, in the following year, Jedidiah made plans to go to London.

Making the 150 mile journey on foot (and counting the blades of grass on the way, said his friends), he agreed to demonstrate his numerical powers to members of the Royal Society which included leading mathematicians of the day. All were astonished to find that Jedidiah knew of no short cuts to use in his calculations. For example, when multiplying by 100, he factorised and multiplied by 5 and then 20 instead of simply adding two noughts.

His only interest in a visit to the theatre to see Garrick in *Richard the Third* was to count the number of words spoken by the actors and the steps in the dances.

Jedidiah's main ambition while in London was to see the king but George II and the Royal Family had removed to Kensington before he arrived in the capital so he set out, disconsolately, to return to Elmton. There he continued to live and to work on the land for the rest of his life.

At the age of 57 he was persuaded to have his portrait painted but he found the sittings tedious and passed the time in reckoning how long he had lived, in seconds.

There is a legend that Jedidiah predicted the time of his death and it is said that he called on the Duke of Portland at Welbeck to say farewell. 'I shall die next Thursday,' he informed His Grace who suspected him of drinking and ordered his servants to prevent Jedidiah from having any beer as his brain seemed to be affected. Jedidiah said goodbye to all his friends and, on the following Thursday returned from work as usual, sat down and ate his dinner and immediately died in his chair.

He was buried in Elmton churchyard on March 5th 1772 but the exact position of his grave is unknown. His portrait, the only memorial to this human calculator, hangs in the vestry of the present church.

Murder
in Winnats Pass

THE village of Peak Forest in north west Derbyshire appears to belie its name. Situated five miles from Buxton and four miles from Chapel-en-le-Frith, it does not comply with the modern definition of a forest which is a region covered in trees. But the name 'forest' used to be given to any wild, unenclosed part of the country and Peak Forest', an exposed bleak place with very few trees, qualifies for this interpretation.

This isolated village was remote and almost unknown to the rest of England, but during the 17th and 18th centuries, Peak Forest achieved fame, even notoriety, as the English Gretna Green, where couples could be married instantly without parental consent or the previous calling of banns.

In 1657 Christiana, Countess of Devonshire, built a chapel there to express her loyalty to the executed King Charles the First. The minister, whose title was 'Principal Official and Judge in Spiritualities in the Peculiar Court of Peak Forest', had the arbitrary right to prove wills, to perform weddings and to issue marriage licences at any time on any day of the year.

On a stipend of £100 a year, he enjoyed these privileges because the King Charles chapel, as it was called, was a free chapelry situated within the royal forest and outside the jurisdiction of the bishop. He was often awakened during the night to officiate at a marriage before the runaway bride and bridegroom could be apprehended.

Most eloping couples came from within a radius of 150 miles

but a special register was kept for foreign weddings (couples not resident in the County of Derby) and the chapel became so well known that an average of 80 couples a year were joined in matrimony at Derbyshire's Gretna Green and, in 1745, 105 weddings were solemnised there. A special wooden seal was used to stamp the marriage certificate.

In 1748 a wealthy young couple from Scotland made the journey on horseback to Derbyshire. Allan and Clara, whose surnames are unknown, intended to take advantage of the ceremony at Peak Forest which needed no preliminary notification.

Their first night in the county was at Stoney Middleton where they spent the night at the Royal Oak inn. It was here, according to legend, that Clara had a terrifying dream in which she saw her lover dragged from his horse and murdered. So distressed was she next morning that she spoke of returning home but Allan succeeded in reassuring her and they took the road to Castleton. At one of the inns there they rested their horses and found refreshment.

The landlord, impressed by the couple's well-to-do appearance, ejected four drunken lead miners who were occupying one of the public rooms in order to make more accommodation for his affluent guests.

As the runaways mounted and set off once more, the resentful ruffians took note of their highly bred horses and Allan's bulging saddle-bag and they listened as the landlord gave directions for the shortest route to Peak Forest which was through the Winnats Pass.

The name 'Winnats' is a corruption of Windygates and this wild ravine road running between the steep mountain sides was a popular haunt of brigands and highwaymen.

Allan and Clara were never seen again. Four days later, their horses were found wandering in the pass and though murder was suspected nobody was apprehended for the crime.

Many years afterwards, in the process of sinking an engine shaft in the Winnats, the skeletons of the young lovers were unearthed, wrapped in a sack. They were hastily reburied in the churchyard at Castleton but still the identity of the murderers remained a mystery.

Some twenty years after Allan and Clara met their deaths a miner named James Ashton made a confession on his deathbed. He had suffered a long and painful illness but admitted he was unable to die until he had relieved his conscience by revealing full details of the crime in which he had taken part. To the Vicar of Castleton he described how he and three other miners had followed the young couple as they picked their way along the rock strewn track of the Winnats Pass. The four rogues dragged them from their horses and hacked them to death, one after the other, with pickaxes. As Clara watched her lover being so brutally murdered, she pleaded with the men to spare her life but they showed her no mercy and she was killed in the same way.

After dividing among them the possessions of the bridal pair which included £200 in money, the men placed the mutilated bodies in a sack before burying them and hastily departed.

Ashton also spoke of the misfortunes which had overtaken his accomplices in the following years. One of them was crushed to death by a fall of rock in the Winnats Pass quite close to the scene of the crime, one hanged himself and the third died insane. Ashton, himself, died soon after making his confession.

It is said that the ghosts of the murdered couple, begging for mercy, still appear when the wind howls through the gorge.

Clara's saddle may be seen in the Speedwell cavern at the foot of the Winnats Pass. This is an old lead mine which has three feet of water in its tunnels allowing visitors to make a tour of it by boat. The deepest cave open to the public in Britain, it includes a vast, natural cavern known as the Bottomless Pit.

By an Act of Parliament in 1804 marriages at Peak Forest chapel were made illegal. The reason given was that they had become 'productive of bad consequences'. The chapel was demolished in the 1870s and, a few years later, the present church was built some 20 yards away, the cost being defrayed by the 7th Duke of Devonshire and called the Church of King Charles the Martyr.

Couples can still be married in the present church without banns being previously called. The only stipulation is that either the bride or the bridegroom must have been resident in the village for at least fifteen days.

The Headstrong Heiress

'**M**Y Jewel', the Countess of Shrewsbury called her granddaughter, Arbella Stuart, whom she hoped would one day occupy the throne of England.

The countess, known as 'Bess of Hardwick', maintained a lifelong ambition to found a family dynasty and she married off her sons and daughters with this end in view. But it was her granddaughter for whom Bess fostered the highest hopes and who brought her the most bitter disappointment.

In 1574, Margaret, Countess of Lennox, mother of Mary Queeen of Scots' murdered husband, Darnley, travelled from London to her estates in Yorkshire, accompanied by her only surviving son, Charles Stuart. The journey had been granted by Queen Elizabeth I only on condition that she and her son did not call at Chatsworth where Mary Queen of Scots, the countess's daughter in law, was imprisoned in the care of Bess's fourth husband, the Earl of Shrewsbury.

On their return, Bess invited the Lennoxes to break their journey at Rufford Abbey in Nottinghamshire, one of Shrewsbury's many seats in the Midlands. There, accompanied by her last unmarried daughter, Elizabeth Cavendish, Bess received them.

Charles Stuart resembled his brother, Henry Darnley, in that he possessed much superficial charm. Elizabeth fell under his spell and, in his mother's words, the 19 year old boy 'entangled himself so he could have none other', and a wedding was hastily arranged, taking place in the Rufford Abbey chapel.

As Charles Stuart was in the line of succession, being a descendant of King Henry VII, the queen's approval should have been sought for his betrothal. When her Majesty learned of the marriage, she was furious and ordered the two countesses to the Tower. The newly weds were placed under house arrest at Hackney. Bess, however, was released in time for the birth of Elizabeth's baby daughter, Arbella, in the autumn of 1575.

Before Arbella was a year old, her father died of consumption. Elizabeth, grieving for her husband, gave the child little attention and when, in 1582, Elizabeth died suddenly during the Twelfth Night celebrations at Sheffield Manor, Arbella's upbringing was entirely in the hands of her grandmother, Bess of Hardwick.

Bess looked upon Arbella as the rightful heiress to the throne of England and set about having her trained in a manner suitable for a future queen. The most highly qualified tutors were appointed for her education. Lessons in Greek and Latin, music and dancing continued whether she was in residence at Chatsworth, Hardwick, Wingfield or Sheffield. At the age of seven, she was able to compose an excellent letter in French.

A painting of Arbella, aged 23 months, in Hardwick Hall depicts a plump, bejewelled child, described by Bess as 'of great towardness'. A later portrait shows a well-made girl who was far from beautiful but was known to be quick witted and headstrong.

Mary Queen of Scots spent a great deal of time with the child until she became aware of Bess's plan for Arbella to succeed Queen Elizabeth. Then she was full of indignation.

'Nothing has alienated the countess from me more', she wrote, 'than the vain hope she has conceived of setting the crown of England on the head of her granddaughter.'

In 1587 Arbella was summoned to court when Queen Elizabeth had plans for her to become betrothed to the Duke of Parma's son in order to ensure peace with Spain. But this came to nothing.

The following year Arbella was again at court and 'dined in the presence' but this time the pomp and flattery went to her head. After the execution of Mary Queen of Scots when Arbella became next in line for the throne following her cousin King James of Scotland, Bess demanded that her granddaughter be treated as a princess of the blood royal and her relatives were ordered to curtsey to her and address her as 'Highness'. Consequently, the thirteen year old girl insisted on taking precedence over the queen's ladies whereupon she was sharply rebuked by Her Majesty and sent back to Derbyshire.

The next few years were spent at Wingfield Manor and then Bess made her last expedition to London, taking Arbella with her and accompanied by her sons, William and Charles, together with their wives and attendants.

Under the eye of her grandmother, Arbella's behaviour was more seemly and, when Bess returned to Derbyshire, her granddaughter was invited to remain at court.

She returned to Hardwick later in the year and, not long after she arrived, Bess was warned that attempts to kidnap Arbella had been threatened. Bess wrote assuring Lord Cecil of the girl's safety. 'I see her almost every hour of the day,' she told him. Nevertheless, she took Arbella to Chatsworth for greater security. When they moved into the newly built Hardwick Hall, Arbella had her own staff and apartments but she still slept in her grandmother's bedchamber.

During the next few years Bess gave Arbella many presents of money and jewellery. But life with an old lady and only books for companions was dull and frustrating for the vivacious girl. Queen Elizabeth appeared to have forgotten her existence. Marriage seemed the only means of escape from an intolerable situation so, at the age of 27, Arbella decided to find a husband for herself.

She persuaded John Dodderidge, one of Bess's old retainers, to take a message to the Earl of Hertford in London, proposing herself in marriage to the earl's grandson, Edward Seymour, aged 16. She also suggested that Edward should visit Hardwick on the pretext of buying land so she could look him over. Dodderidge made the journey to the capital in five days and, on his knees, duly delivered the message to the earl who had him taken before the Council next morning to repeat it to the members. Suspecting that Arbella's proposal was part of a Catholic plot, Sir Henry Bronker was despatched to Hardwick to investigate.

In consternation, Arbella gave him a garbled, contradictory account of the episode and accused old Dodderidge of lying. Bronker then required her to set down the facts in writing which she did but produced a statement which he called, 'confused, obscure and, in truth, ridiculous.' Bronker returned to London carrying with him a letter from Bess in which she protested her ignorance of her granddaughter's hare-brained scheme and begged Queen Elizabeth to take the girl off her hands or find her a husband. Her Majesty's reply directed only that Arbella must remain at Hardwick and be more carefully guarded.

Then followed a distressing time for the old countess; her granddaughter openly defying her, making hysterical threats to escape and dropping wild hints about a secret lover. At one stage Arbella went on a hunger strike.

'She is so wilfully bent', wrote Bess in yet another letter begging to be relieved of the troublesome girl, and added, 'A few more weeks as I have suffered of late will make an end of me.'

When Bess's 'bad son', Henry Cavendish, who was always eager to spite his mother, turned up at the gates of Hardwick with a party of horsemen in an attempt to rescue Arbella, the girl had to be forcibly restrained by Bess's servants from joining him and he finally departed. After this incident, Bronker paid a further visit to Hardwick and found Bess in utter despair. By now, he was beginning to doubt Arbella's sanity and recommended that she be removed from her grandmother's care. She was hurriedly sent to Wrest Park in Bedfordshire in charge of the Earl of Kent.

During this time, Queen Elizabeth lay dying. With a nod, she indicated that King James of Scotland, son of Queen Mary, was to be her successor, thus putting an end to Bess's hopes for Arbella who, it must be said, had never entertained any desire to be queen.

Arbella now became friendly with King James's wife, Queen Anne, and was invited to live at court. She took a prominent part in the coronation and, soon afterwards, travelled to Derbyshire carrying a letter from the king asking Bess to consider making a reconciliation with her granddaughter.

As a result of this visit, Arbella was reinstated in Bess's will from which she had been removed on account of her appalling behaviour. Bess died on 13th February 1608 and with her grandmother's legacy, Arbella bought a house in Blackfriars.

At thirty-five and still unmarried, Arbella again approached the Seymour family for a husband. This time the prospective bridegroom was Edward's younger brother, William, aged twenty-two. After a brief courtship, they were married at Greenwich, assuring the minister and six witnesses that the king had given his consent.

When King James heard of the marriage, William was arrested and sent to the Tower and Arbella was despatched to Lambeth in the charge of Sir Thomas Parry. Fearing the risk of Arbella having children who might be claimants to the throne, James ordered her removal to Durham.

But Arbella had other plans. Disguising herself as a man, she rode fourteen miles to Blackwall where she had asked William to meet her. His luggage arrived with a servant but he was delayed. Not daring to linger, Arbella made her way to Leigh where a French boat was waiting as she had ordered. It eventually set sail with her for Calais. In the meantime William arrived too late to join his wife and paid £40 to cross the Channel in a collier. When a proclamation was sent out for Arbella's arrest, the French boat was soon intercepted and all those connected with the escapade were put in the Tower.

Languishing in captivity, month after month, Arbella lost the will to live and died in 1615. A post mortem showed that she had, in fact, starved herself to death.

She was buried in Westminster Abbey in the vault containing the body of Mary Queen of Scots.

A Noble
Ménage à Trois

GEORGIANA, daughter of Earl and Countess Spencer who were ancestors of Diana, Princess of Wales, was born on 7th June 1757. She was brought up at Althorp in Northamptonshire together with her younger sister, Harriet, and brother, George John, known to everyone as 'Althorp'.

The girls were educated at home by their mother, a pious woman of strong character whose firm discipline and practical counselling earned their deep respect and life-long devotion.

Poets, writers, statesmen and noblemen were constant visitors at Althorp and among them was the wealthy young Duke of Devonshire who, in 1774, requested Georgiana's hand in marriage. Not yet 17 and, according to her contemporaries, 'pronouncedly giddy though unbelievably lovely', Georgiana could not have hoped for a better match and she became the Duchess of Devonshire just before her 17th birthday.

The Duke was 24 and described as 'humourless and passionless'. Easily bored, he was lethargic to a degree in contrast to the vivacious and impulsive Duchess who was obliged to restrain her demonstrativeness as the Duke was horrified by any show of affection.

The first few months of their married life were spent at Chatsworth with short spells at Hardwick where Georgiana endeared herself to both the indoor and outdoor staff by her generosity and consideration. She charmed everyone by her captivating manner and the warmth of her personality, her mother describing her as 'amiable and innocent but too fond of dissipation.'

On moving to Devonshire House in London for the Season, Georgiana immediately became a leader of fashion and the centre of that brilliant circle of society people who had adopted an extravagant lifestyle. The hectic pace of Georgiana's social life stemmed from the coldness and indifference she met with in her husband and from her inability to manage money. Longing to be loved and cherished, she learned to subdue her emotions and threw herself into a frivolous existence which included nights of reckless gambling. In spite of dire warnings from her mother she soon accumulated an alarming number of debts and, within a few months of her marriage, admitted that she owed the local tradespeople more than £1,600.

Georgiana's letters to her mother reveal a marked talent for writing. She often included lines of spontaneously written verse or relapsed into French, pouring out her thoughts and apologising for her laziness in getting up in the mornings which her mother had criticised and, more often than not, ending with a request for a loan of money. The Sylph, a novel published anonymously in 1779, was autobiographical and Georgiana never denied its authorship. The heroine, like herself, lived in 'a constant bustle without having anything to do'.

In 1775 Georgiana had the first of several miscarriages which her father attributed to all her 'racketing' and begged her to live more prudently. Some time later, she discovered that the Duke had an illegitimate daughter, Charlotte Williams, born about the time of their marriage. Georgiana showed no resentment at this revelation but arranged for the child's upbringing and education.

A visit to Bath with the Duke in May 1782 saw the beginning of an association which was to affect both their lives for there they met Lady Elizabeth Foster. Separated from her husband who had taken their two sons away with him to Ireland where he was an MP, Lady Elizabeth was described as a 'truly feminine woman, though sophisticated enough'. Certainly she was less naive than Georgiana and soon managed to ingratiate herself into the Devonshire household, admired and loved by both the Duke and Duchess. For the next twenty years she remained Georgiana's trusted friend and confidante and, at the same time, the Duke's mistress.

When Georgiana found herself with child once more, it was Lady Elizabeth, or 'Bess' as she was now called, who nursed her through the first trying months of her pregnancy.

Because Bess was troubled by a persistent cough, it was decided that she must go abroad for the sake of her health and, having been appointed as governess to the Duke's illegitimate daughter, she took the child with her, all expenses being paid by the Duke.

Georgiana's first child was born on 12th July 1783, – not the longed for heir but a girl named Georgiana Dorothy whom her mother said she 'would not change for ten sons'. She was known as 'Little G'.

In spite of Georgiana's happiness in her new daughter, she was still engulfed by enormous gambling debts, borrowing from all and sundry and particularly from Thomas Coutts, the banker, who lent her vast sums accompanied by fatherly advice urging her to curb her indiscretions.

Bess returned to Chatsworth for a short spell but, at the end of 1784, found it necessary to go abroad again. This time Bess was absent for about 18 months and she left in France a daughter by the Duke, born on 16th August 1785. The child was named Caroline St. Jules. A fortnight later, on August 29th, Georgiana gave birth to a second daughter, Harriet, known all her life as Harry-O.

Bess returned to England in the summer of 1786 and was met by the Duke. 'Oh, heavens, such moments do indeed efface past sorrows', she confided to her diary and quickly resumed her place in the Devonshire household and in society. By the beginning of 1788, however, she prepared to make another trip to the continent. Georgiana and the Duke travelled with her to Dover where the last goodbyes were said. 'His last look drew my soul after him,' she wrote. 'Oh, why could I not love him without crime? Why cannot I be his without sin?'. Bess was, in fact, six months pregnant and, this time, Georgiana was aware of the situation.

Bess settled in Rouen where the Duke sent an accoucheur to attend her. On 26th May 1788 the Duke's first son, though not his heir, was born and named Augustus Clifford, the latter being one of the Duke's titles.

Meanwhile Georgiana continued to lose heavily at the gambling tables, borrowing from Sir Richard Arkwright of Cromford and many others. In a letter to Thomas Coutts, her 'dear friend', she promised to reveal the amount of her debts to the Duke after the hoped for heir she was expecting was born. When this important event took place, she failed to make the promised confession and admitted to Coutts that she owed more than £60,000.

It was after 16 years of married life that Georgiana finally produced the Devonshire heir, the Marquess of Hartington, and he was born in Paris. In the summer of 1789, the Duke and Duchess of Devonshire, Lady Elizabeth Foster, Charlotte Williams and a host of servants set out for a prolonged holiday in Spa, a popular watering place in Belgium. Little G. and Harry-O were left in the care of their grandmother. The purpose of this expedition was to find a cure for the Duke's gout and to promote Georgiana's fertility. In Paris a French couple called Nagel were put in charge of Charlotte and they later became responsible for Caroline St. Jules and the latest arrival, Augustus Clifford. By the time the Devonshires were ready to return home, it was established that Georgiana was pregnant and the Duke decided it was too risky for her to make the journey in her condition. Early in 1790, therefore, Lady Spencer joined the party with the two little girls, taking with her a governess, a doctor and more servants.

Hartington was born on 21st May 1790. Thus, it was said, 'Georgiana redeemed the reproach that had shadowed her life'.

In spite of having a number of people to witness the event and a signed statement from the doctor who delivered the child, there was a rumour, persisting for years, that Hartington was Bess's son.

It was soon after their return to England that Georgiana's sister, Harriet, was taken ill and lost the use of her left arm and leg. Georgiana accompanied her to Bath where the planned short holiday extended to some months.

Hardly had they settled in Bath when Georgiana embarked on a passionate affair with Charles Grey whom she had known for some time and who had been a clandestine visitor at Devonshire House in the Duke's absence. Aged 27, Grey was a brilliant statesman and was Prime Minister from 1830 to 1834. The result was that Georgiana became pregnant and, when the Duke discovered this, he banished her abroad forthwith, even though he had, himself, fathered at least three bastards. In some aristocratic families of that period, it was considered permissible for a wife to indulge in an extramarital affair so long as she had already supplied her husband with an heir. Obviously the Duke of Devonshire did not subscribe to this attitude.

Giving her reason for leaving England as the necessity to accompany her sister whose doctors had ordered her abroad for her health, Georgiana crossed to France with Harriet and Bess and settled for a time in Paris. There, on 20th February 1792, she gave birth to Grey's daughter who was named Eliza Courtney. Far from receiving any moral support from Charles Grey, his brief notes indicate that the whole episode should be quickly forgotten. The child was brought up by Grey's family, Georgiana being allowed to see her only infrequently and strictly as a visitor.

Georgiana wrote numerous letters to the Duke pleading with him to allow her to return home and to the children begging them not to forget her but it was not until late in 1793 that the Duke relented and she was joyfully reunited with her two little girls although Hartington, naturally, treated her as a stranger. It was reported that she received a warm welcome from the Duke on her arrival at Devonshire House and he gave a servants' ball in her honour.

It was a somewhat subdued Georgiana who took up the threads of her social life once more. Georgiana's constant debts continued to escalate, the Duke of Bedford, on one occasion, lending her £6,000 and Thomas Coutts continuing to respond to her pleas to get her 'out of a scrape'. In 1804, it was rumoured that the Duke had arranged for £40,000 of what she owed to be paid off but at that time the total sum was estimated at over £100,000.

In late 1805, still suffering from headaches caused by persistent eye trouble, Georgiana was found to have gallstones and the various treatments she received from a succession of doctors sound like horrific tortures. Her head was shaved, leeches were applied to her eyeball and blisters to her scalp. She took large quantities of opium for the pain. 'This beautiful duchess,' commented a visitor, 'now looks bald and barely human.'

Her daughter, Harriet never left her bedside and on March 30th she finally died after a lingering illness of indescribable agony. She was in her 49th year.

On April 5th, Georgiana's body was taken from Devonshire House in London to be interred in the family vault at Edensor, close by Chatsworth. The *Morning Chronicle* proclaimed that 'never was the death of any human being more universally lamented'. The Prince of Wales called it 'a loss and calamity beyond all sufferance'.

'Was that all?' exclaimed the Duke on hearing the amount of her debts. 'Why, oh why did she not tell me?'

In October 1809, the Duke of Devonshire married Lady Elizabeth Foster, explaining that there was 'an impropriety in Lady Elizabeth living in his house on any other terms'. When the Duke died in 1811, the Duchess Elizabeth left England, provided for by an allowance from Hartington, now the 6th Duke of Devonshire. She died in Rome in 1824.

The Plague
at Eyam

THAT the secluded village of Eyam, situated among the hills of Derbyshire's Peakland, should have been visited by a pestilential disease which had mainly occurred only in large cities was a surprise to everyone in the Midlands.

Called the Bubonic Plague, it was characterised by swollen, inflamed lymphatic glands of different sizes, usually in or near the groin but, occasionally, in the armpit. Vomiting was accompanied by fever and delirium and a purple blotch appearing on the chest indicated that death was inevitable.

The nursery rhyme, 'Ring o' Roses' recalled the stages of the disease, the ring being the purple rash, the pocket of posies the nosegay of aromatic herbs carried as a preventative, 'atishoo' described the shivering and sneezing and 'all fall down' was the final collapse. The infection was transferred by fleas from rats to humans, the germs carried in clothes and bedding existing for months.

There were numerous treatments recommended for the disease, one by an 'Approved Physitian' directing, 'If there doe a botch appear, take a Pigeon and pluke the feathers off her tail, very bare, and set her tail to the sore, and shee will draw out the venome until shee die'. Added advice from the medical profession, somewhat unnecessary in the circumstances, one would think, warned, 'All should studiously avoid dancing, running, leaping about, lechery and bathing'.

At the beginning of September, 1665, a journeyman tailor named George Viccars lodged in Eyam with Mary Cooper, a widow, and her two sons who lived in what is now called the 'Plague Cottage' near the church. Viccars received a parcel from London containing samples of cloth which were found to be damp and he spread them before the fire to dry.

Within a few days he was taken ill and died and, a fortnight later, one of Mrs Cooper's sons died having shown similar symptoms. Four more deaths occurred before the end of September and, by this time it was evident that the village was in the cruel grasp of the Plague. Another 23 inhabitants perished during October but, when only seven people died in November, it was hoped that the wintry conditions might suppress the infection. However, between December and the following May, fifty deaths were recorded and with the onset of warmer weather, the number of people stricken with the disease increased alarmingly.

By this time many wealthy inhabitants had left the village in haste, including the Bradshaw family from the Hall, and a number of villagers built temporary huts in which to live on the outskirts.

The rector, the Rev William Mompesson, now urged his wife, Katherine, to take their children, George and Margaret, to stay with relatives in order to escape from the danger but, although she agreed to let the children go, she insisted on staying by her husband's side. With the help of his predecessor, the Rev Thomas Stanley, who had been ejected from the living after the Restoration on account of his Puritanical leanings, Mompesson persuaded his parishioners to remain in the village rather than spread the infection by fleeing to other places. All but two people accepted this restriction. In fact, residents of Eyam were distinctly unwelcome in any other town or village and Sheffield, Bakewell and Tideswell employed sentries to refuse entry to anyone suspected of coming from Eyam.

One woman was brave enough to venture to Tideswell and managed to evade the sentry there but was soon recognised.

'The Plague, the Plague – a woman from Eyam,' went up the cry and she was pursued out of the town by an angry mob throwing at her stones, turf and all kinds of missiles.

The Earl of Devonshire undertook to see that the isolated village was provided with food, clothes and medical supplies. On the boundary was a trough of water, now called 'Mompesson's Well', which had vinegar added to it as a disinfectant, and money in payment was placed in it.

Mompesson then decided to close the church and, preaching from a rock, he held services in the Delph, a valley nearby, while the ever dwindling congregation sat on the grass, widely spaced in order to avoid infection. This place became known as Cucklet Church and here the Plague Commemoration Service is held annually.

The churchyard overflowed. It was no longer possible to give the victims a decent burial for there was no time to make coffins or linger over funeral rites. With a hasty prayer, many were buried where they fell.

A man named Marshall Howe had recovered from a mild attack of the disease and was therefore immune against a similar infection. He made a bargain with the villagers, agreeing to bury the dead in exchange for their possessions. A man of powerful physique, he dug shallow graves in gardens, on the common and on the hillsides. Eager to bury the corpses and help himself to their belongings, he once dragged a man from his bed in order to consign him to a grave he had newly dug. But the 'corpse' cried out in protest and, in a panic, Marshall dropped him down the stairs and ran. This victim was one of the few who made a recovery.

Nineteen deaths were recorded in June but, in July, the number of victims rose by 56. Richard Talbot of Riley Farm was the village blacksmith. On July 5th two of his daughters died of the epidemic, then, one after another, the rest of the family succumbed. Father, mother, two sons and another daughter all died in the same month and were buried on the site of the farm.

Shortly after the tragedy of the Talbot family, the Hancocks who lived nearby were stricken. The father, 3 sons and 3 daughters all died within eight days and all were buried by the mother who then left the village to join her one remaining son who was living in Sheffield. The burial place of the Hancocks is in a field about ¼ mile east of the village. Known as the 'Riley Graves', they include a table monument recording the death of John Hancock on August 7th and six headstones in memory of his sons and daughters. A rough stone wall, heart shaped, was built to protect the graves and surrounds them.

In August a total of 77 people died and among them was Katherine Mompesson, the rector's wife. Already suffering from tuberculosis, she was unsparing in her ministrations to the despairing community. One evening Mompesson took her for a walk in the fresh air, away from the stench of sickness and dead bodies.

'Oh, Mompesson, the air,' she exclaimed. 'how sweet it smells.' At these words her husband's heart sank for he recognised the imagined scent as a dreaded sign of death. Katherine was buried on August 25th 1666, the 200th victim.

Mompesson wrote to his children telling them of their mother's death and giving touching details of her last hours. 'She is now,' he told them, 'invested with a crown of righteousness.' Since his own death then seemed inevitable, Mompesson set about making his will, appointed executors and 'left the future to God'.

It was near the end of August and Marshall Howe became personally involved in the grief he had witnessed, indifferently, in other families. His wife, Joan, became ill and died and, no sooner had he buried her than his son fell a victim to the fatal disease. September saw the deaths of 24 more inhabitants and, in October there were 14 more.

After an interment on November 1st, the people waited for a continuation of the pestilence but none came. The few inhabitants left had no heart for anything but marking the graves with stones in order to identify them and wondering what the future held. Gardens and farmland were neglected and overgrown.

'Our town,' wrote Mompesson to a friend, 'is become a Golgotha, a place of the skull', for it was said that every remaining resident was a mourner and every house had been a mortuary. Since April 1664 when he had become the incumbent at Eyam, 260 of his parishioners had perished.

Mompesson supervised a series of bonfires on which clothing, bedding, furniture and anything that could harbour germs was burnt. Houses were fumigated and the residents were encouraged to make an effort in building a new life.

Three years afterwards Mompesson was appointed to the living of Eakring in Nottinghamshire but the parishioners there refused to allow him to use the church pulpit so he preached under a tree called 'Pulpit Ash'. Until they were certain he was free from infection, they insisted that he lived in a hut in Rufford Park.

He died on March 7th 1708 and was buried in Eakring church where his memorial is a stained glass window. His portrait in oils can be seen in Southwell Minster.

Every year, on the last Sunday in August, a service of homage to the Reverend William Mompesson and the Eyam martyrs is held at Cucklet Delph.

Castleton Garland Day

IN the centre of the High Peak of Derbyshire is the old village of Castleton surrounded by hills on which it was the custom, on Easter Sunday morning, for crowds of people to stand looking towards the east as they waited to see the sun 'come up dancing' as it rose. Castleton is famous for its caverns, many of them open to the public, which are some of the most spectacular in Europe. High above the village stand the ruins of Peveril Castle, immortalised by Sir Walter Scott's *Peveril of the Peak*. In the parish church of St Edmund can be seen a 'Breeches Bible', dated 1611.

The ancient ceremony known as Castleton Garland Day began as an ancient fertility rite and was believed to encourage the early onset of Summer. Before the Commonwealth period after the Civil War it took place on May Day (May 1st) but, on Cromwell's orders, it was discontinued. Revived after the Restoration in 1680 when Charles II ascended the throne, it has been held ever since on May 29th to mark the occasion when, as a fugitive from Parliamentary troops, he hid in the Boscobel Oak in Shropshire in 1651. For this reason, May 29th soon became known locally as Oak and Nettle day when children on their way to school took the precaution of wearing a spray of oak leaves to prevent their legs being stung by older boys who carried bunches of stinging nettles and called out, 'Show us yer oak'.

This is the day on which the Garland King makes a tour of the village on horseback, the Garland Queen riding, sidesaddle, behind him. The splendid shire horse which carried the king year after year died some time ago and now a substitute from Sheffield or Darley Dale enjoys the honour.

The king and queen are both dressed in Stuart costume and the queen is now a young woman. Before 1956 a man took the part, wearing female clothes and a veil over his head as it was thought that no woman was strong enough to control a horse surrounded by the various noises of shouting, cheering, singing and band playing. But in recent years queens have been young women and have managed their mounts as successfully as any males. A bell shaped wooden cage decorated with wild flowers and foliage covers the king's head and shoulders. This is The Garland and, on top, is a special bunch of garden flowers, known as the Queen's Posy.

Following their Majesties is the Castleton Silver Band and then comes a bevy of schoolgirls all dressed in white and carrying white flowers. These girls have, for some years, superseded the original troupe of all-male Morris Dancers whose music was customarily provided by two fiddles and a flute. A troop of boy scouts brings up the rear.

Proceeding through the village, halts are made at six public houses, the girls performing a traditional country dance outside each one. At the Market Place they dance the Castleton Morris Dance, the Garland tune being played in accompaniment while onlookers sing vigorously its incomprehensible words.

'Ah dunna know, ah dunna care what they do in Bradder (Bradwell),

Piece o' beef an' an owd cow's yead an' a puddin' baked in a lantern'.

This 'song' is said to have some connection with the Cornish Floral Dance and may have been brought into the county by Cornish tin miners who came centuries ago, to work in the Derbyshire lead mines.

The procession comes to an end at the church gates where

the final part of the ceremony takes place and the king rides into the churchyard. The Garland which is almost three feet high and weighs around 56 lbs is lifted from his shoulders. The queen's posy is removed and is later placed on the village War Memorial while the Last Post is sounded in memory of the Castleton men who gave their lives in the two world wars. The Garland is then hoisted on to one of the eight pinnacles of the church tower where it remains until its flowers have faded when it is taken down and saved for the following year.

The
Blind Heretic
of Derby

JOAN Waste and her twin brother, Roger, were born in the parish of All Hallows, Derby in 1534. A puny pair, they were baptised after three days because it was feared that they might not survive. By the time they were a month old, however, they were both thriving but their mother was beginning to suspect that Joan's eyesight was defective. Before long, it was established that she was totally blind.

Not an uncommon condition in those days, it was accepted with resignation by her parents. William Waste, the twins' father, was a barber and rope maker, neither occupation affording him more than a meagre living so the fee for the attention of a qualified physician would have been impossible to find. Nevertheless, friends and relations recommended a variety of remedies, all of which were tried to no avail. They bathed the baby's eyes with her own urine, applied to them a noxious lotion containing crushed blow-flies, insects thought to have unusually penetrating sight, and fetched water with supposedly curative properties from Saint Alkmund's well in which to bath her. As a last resort, it was arranged for a puppy, still suckling, to be killed and have its eyes removed in the hope that its sight might be transferred to the blind infant. At length,

44

William and his wife became convinced that their child's affliction was the will of God though they could not refrain from wondering what sin they had committed that deserved such a punishment.

Growing up in a world of darkness, Joan relied on her brother to guide and protect her whenever she ventured from the safety of their home and, while quite young, she was allowed to help him in turning the heavy wheel for their father as he made ropes and twine. Also, having developed a keen sense of touch, Joan learnt early to knit and she spent many hours a day making hose and the woollen sleeves for doublets worn by men at that period.

By the time Joan reached her teens, she was able to find her way around most parts of the town, groping along its narrow streets and passage ways. A growing interest in religion caused her to make her way, as often as possible, to one of the Derby churches and she usually managed to be present at the daily service at All Hallows or else at Saint Michael's nearby.

Having an excellent memory, Joan became familiar with the Protestant prayers and psalms and could repeat whole sections of the bible. By carefully saving every penny she made from her knitting, she was able to buy a copy of the New Testament. Disappointed that her brother was unable to make out more than a few words of the stories it contained, she constantly sought someone who could read to her from the gospels, sometimes offering a penny for such a favour.

One of Joan's favourite expeditions was to the town gaol, built across a brook in the Cornmarket. Visitors were allowed to take gifts of food or drink to those prisoners detained for only minor offences. There she struck up a friendship with John Hurt, an old man serving a sentence for debt, who would willingly read to her in exchange for a good sized oatcake in payment. The Parish Clerk of All Hallows also could sometimes be persuaded to read a chapter for her and she was soon conversant with all the books of the New Testament.

Joan was nineteen when Mary Tudor ascended the English

throne. A fanatical Roman Catholic, the Queen was well known for her hatred of the Protestant religion. Called 'Bloody Mary', she cast aside the English prayer book and persecuted anyone who denied the Catholic faith.

In spite of many warnings, Joan openly maintained her Protestant beliefs and made no secret of her aversion to Popery. When her parents died a year or two later, she continued to live contentedly with her brother but some of the neighbours accused her of being a heretic. They sent her name to the Bishop of Lichfield, Doctor Ralph Barnes who, on his next visit to Derby called Joan up for questioning.

Accompanying her to All Hallows church, Roger watched as his sightless sister stood calmly before the Bishop. She answered all his questions and frankly admitted that she could not believe in transubstantiation. This asserts that the bread and wine received at the Communion service actually changes into the body and blood of Christ. 'Even at the Last Supper,' said Joan, 'the bread and wine were only representative and could not have been converted in the manner acknowledged by the Catholic church.'

Reluctant to condemn 'this poor, blind, unlearned woman' as he called her, the bishop allowed his chancellor to interview Joan in the presence of Sir John Port and Lord Vernon, two members of the Derbyshire gentry. She explained to them that her beliefs were founded on the Holy Scriptures and confessed that she was prepared to die for her faith. When they threatened her with imprisonment, torture and death, she said quietly, 'Do your pleasure,' and so she was found guilty of heresy.

Because it was not within the church's power to put her to death, she was handed over to the town bailiffs, Richard Ward and William Bembridge, who kept her in prison for several weeks. During this time she saw no-one until August 1st 1556 when her brother was directed to take her once more to All Hallows church, now Derby Cathedral.

There she was made to stand before the pulpit while Doctor Draycott preached a sermon in which he accused Joan of being 'not only physically blind but spiritually blind as well'. 'Her body,' he proclaimed, 'will be consumed by fire and her soul will be destroyed in hell.' He impressed on the congregation that it was unlawful to pray for Joan as she was a heretic.

Dr Draycott then ordered the bailiffs to carry out her execution and, muttering that he felt 'great sorrow for her death', he returned to the inn where he was lodging and slept soundly while Joan went to face her martyrdom.

Holding her brother's hand, she left the church, followed by a great crowd of people. They walked down Irongate, crossed the brook at the bottom of Sadlergate and made their way up Abbey Street to the Windmill Pit situated just off the Burton road. Here a large stake had been driven into the ground and pieces of wood were being placed at its base.

As they approached, a man came forward and gently placed his hand on Joan's arm. At this, she fell on her brother's neck and kissed him tenderly.

'Farewell, dear Roger,' she whispered and he could only reply, brokenly, 'God be with you', as his beloved sister was taken from him for ever. Through his tears he watched them tie her to the stake and light a fire beneath her feet. 'Christ have mercy', she cried as the flames crept upwards and women onlookers fell, fainting, to the ground. 'May God forgive them' sobbed Roger and, turning, he put his hands over his ears and stumbled away. Then the fire took possession of Joan's body entirely, rendering her unconscious, and she finally died.

The belief that Joan Waste still haunts the site where she was burnt to death more than 400 years ago, was revived in 1975 when a landslide in Mill Hill Lane, close by, caused tons of earth and rubble to crash down on to the patch of land, still known as the Windmill Pit.

Tradition has it that no kind of vegetation has grown on that spot since Joan's martyrdom took place there.

The
Father of the
Factory System

THE 13th child of impoverished parents, Richard
Arkwright was born in Preston, Lancashire, on 23rd
December 1732. Adopted as a young child by a bachelor uncle
after whom he was named, he resisted every type of schooling
and, as soon as he was old enough, began work as a lather boy
for a local barber. When his uncle died, leaving him a small
legacy, he moved to Bolton and found work with Edward Pollitt,
a peruke maker, who recognised that Richard's engaging
personality would be useful in persuading girls to part with their
tresses. In addition to shaving and wig making, Richard soon
added bloodletting and toothpulling to his attainments and, after
Pollitt died, carried on the business for a time before opening
a shop of his own. This was in a dark cellar, the sign in the
street above advertising, 'The Subterranean Barber – a Clean
Shave for One Penny'. In his spare time Richard experimented
with hair dyes which would withstand sun and rain and
simultaneously carried on a trade in patent medicines.

Becoming affluent, he married a schoolmaster's daughter,
Patience Holt, in 1755 but, soon after his son, Dick, was born,
his wife died, the tragedy precipitating his life long tendency
to asthma. Because of Richard's indifferent health, the business

began to suffer until he met and married Margaret Biggins of Leigh whose personal capital of £400 and her energetic help with the wig making resulted in their trade expanding considerably. Three daughters were born of the union but only one, Susannah, survived.

Soon the Arkwrights could afford to employ a journeyman to work in the shop while Richard travelled round fairs where he bought women's hair. On one of these expeditions, he met John Kay, a clockmaker from Warrington, who encouraged Richard to try to design a cotton spinning machine. Leaving the barber's business in the care of his wife, Arkwright gave himself up solely to working on this invention.

Such experiments were dangerous in a town like Bolton on account of the popular belief that machines caused unemployment so he decided to move. Notwithstanding his wife's fury when told of his intention and the fact that she threw his models out of the window, he departed for Preston and hired a room where Kay soon joined him in setting up the spinning frame. This consisted of two pairs of rollers which passed the thread from one to the other and drew it out to the required thickness to be used as warp. Arkwright and Kay worked in secret and when neighbours, hearing the whirring of the machines at night, spread the story that witchcraft was being practised with 'strange humming noises like the devil tuning his bagpipes', the two men were careful to foster the rumour in order to conceal their activities.

In 1768 Dick took his father the news that trade at the barber's shop was dwindling. Almost penniless by this time, Arkwright quickly sold the shop and his house as well and moved to Nottingham, well away from the rioters who had destroyed Hargreaves's 'Spinning Jenny'. Margaret refused to accompany him and went to live with relatives in Leigh, taking Susannah with her but Dick stayed with his father and, together, they opened a barber's shop in Nottingham, working on the spinning frame at night.

With the new machine finally working satisfactorily,

Arkwright obtained a patent and, supported financially by two wealthy mill owners, Samuel Need and Jedediah Strutt, inventor of the 'Derby Rib' stocking, he built a mill there and carried on a flourishing trade.

Eager to expand, he began to look for a site where water power could be used to drive his machines instead of horses. He decided on Cromford near Matlock where the river Derwent never froze and where there was an abundance of man, woman and child labour to be drawn from the neighbourhood.

Not only did Arkwright build the Upper Mill there but, within a short time, an entire village of cottages had been erected to house his workers. By 1771 more and bigger mills had been built and were working round the clock in shifts, candles being used at night-time. In the year 1776 Arkwright factories were established in Lancashire, Nottinghamshire and Staffordshire as well as in Derbyshire and their employees numbered more than 5,000.

At Cromford, he also built a school, a chapel and an inn, the 'Greyhound', which still stands. He also gained permission for a Saturday market to be held in the village and annual fairs in May and October. When Masson Mill was completed, he had over 800 people in the vicinity working for him, most of the number being women and children for a great many men were employed in the local lead mines.

A benevolent employer, he made strict rules concerning child labour. He did not employ children under the age of ten and took on only those who had learnt to read and write. His mills worked a six day week, leaving Sunday free for attendance at church or chapel. By 1787 there were 22 mills belonging to Arkwright in Derbyshire, all driven by water power, and he still occupied much of his time with the invention of more up to date machines.

Becoming increasingly wealthy, Arkwright began to travel, to entertain and to mix with those called scornfully by Need, his partner, as 'the county folk'. Gratified at being invited to dine at Chatsworth House, he soon discovered that friendship with the Duchess of Devonshire who was an inveterate gambler, led to being asked for the loan of 'a bit o' brass', unknown to the Duke.

As a result of these associations, Arkwright decided that he must do something about his lack of education for he depended on Dick to do all his letter writing. He therefore set aside an hour or two each day for practising writing and spelling and he made sure that Susannah had a good education.

Because of his phenomenal success in the cotton industry, he was forced to maintain a constant fight against opposition and was often involved in disputes regarding the authenticity of his patents. A man called Highs accused Arkwright of copying one of his inventions and, in support of Highs, manufacturers all over England refused to pay royalties due so that he was obliged to prosecute nine of his rivals.

It was at this time that Need retired from the partnership. Strutt took over the mills at Nottingham and Belper and Arkwright, together with Dick, now a partner, was left with the rest.

On the grounds that his improvements in machinery reduced the work available for spinners in their homes, Arkwright was pinpointed for retribution. When a factory belonging to him at Chorley was wrecked by vindictive mobs, he placed his Derbyshire mills in a state of seige and Margaret and Susannah were hurriedly brought over from Leigh.

For some years Arkwright had lived at Rock House in Cromford. Susannah spent her holidays here but his wife, determined not to be affected by his wealth, paid him no more than occasional visits, a young widow in Bakewell supplying him with the affection he needed and with two children. Requiring a more roomy residence in which to entertain on a larger scale, he purchased an estate overlooking the Derwent from William Edward Nightingale, father of Florence, and there he built an imposing mansion. Calling it Willersley Hall, he proceeded to fill it with elaborate furnishings and pictures including a portrait of himself by Joseph Wright.

'Put in t'rollers o't'spinning frame,' he instructed the artist. 'It's them what made me t'brass.'

Just as he was on the point of moving in, a large part of the building was gutted by fire and had to be rebuilt.

When King George III was attacked by a maniac, Arkwright was chosen to present His Majesty with an address of loyalty from the people of Derbyshire. He travelled to London and returned home a knight. Now he was Sir Richard Arkwright of Willersley but his wife steadfastly refused to be known as Lady Margaret or to take part in the celebrations the following year when her husband was made High Sheriff.

It was said that, during his year of office, Sir Richard dressed ostentatiously, disbursed money generously and entertained lavishly. As soon as Willersley was suitable for occupation, he held a large ball there attended by all the notables of the county including the Duchess of Devonshire.

When their father's health began to fail, Dick and Susannah persuaded Margaret to make her home with him permanently. So, until his death, his last days were spent with her, peacefully, beside the river Derwent whose waters had brought him a fortune.

He died on August 3rd 1792 and was buried at Matlock church but in 1797, when Saint Mary's church at Cromford was completed, his remains were transferred there where many members of the Arkwright family were subsequently buried.

The
Padley Martyrs

AFTER the accession of Queen Elizabeth I in 1558, the country reverted to Protestantism and practising Catholics ran the risk of being heavily fined, thrown into prison or even put to death.

Persistent searches of houses belonging to the gentry led to the arrest of Sir Thomas Fitzherbert, the owner of Padley Manor in north Derbyshire, built by the Padley family in the 15th century. Sir Thomas was a staunch Catholic who refused to give up his faith and was therefore consigned to the Fleet Prison in London, leaving his brother, John, to look after his estates. Sir Thomas had no children and John's eldest son, Thomas, was his successor.

In February 1587 Mary Queen of Scots was executed at Fotheringay and when, in July the following year, news came that the Spanish Armada was on its way, Queen Elizabeth realised that many of the Scottish queen's Catholic supporters would favour the enterprise. She therefore instructed Sir George Talbot, 6th Earl of Shrewsbury, who was Earl Marshall of England and Lord Lieutenant of Derbyshire, to commit all prominent Roman Catholics to prison.

Aged sixty and gout ridden, the Earl, who was Bess of Hardwick's husband, issued an order for the search of every Papist in the county and sent a magistrate to Padley Manor with orders to arrest John Fitzherbert. Twenty three people, all suspect, were found there on this occasion but John was not there and no arrests were made. John's son, Thomas, eager to inherit his uncle's estates, sent word to the Earl of Shrewsbury a few weeks later that his father was then at Padley.

Wasting no time, the Earl set out from Sheffield Castle early on the morning of July 12th 1558. Accompanied by a party of men, he rode to Padley and made a raid on the Manor House.

John Fitzherbert, his second son, Anthony, three of his daughters and ten serving men were captured with Thomas's help. Two Roman Catholic priests, Nicholas Garlick, a Tideswell schoolmaster, and Robert Ludlam, a Yorkshireman, were found hiding in a 'priest hole', constructed as a secret hiding place for a Catholic priest in time of persecution. In this case it was a hollow chimney. The priests had, a short time before, been celebrating Mass in the chapel and they were immediately arrested.

Only twelve days later, Ludlam and Garlick, together with Richard Sympson who joined them in Derby gaol, being also guilty of performing the offices of a priest, were hanged, drawn and quartered in Derby Market Place. The death sentence at their trial directed, 'your heads be severed from your bodies; your privy members be cut off; your bowels be taken out and burned before your faces'.

Crowds of onlookers watched these gruesome proceedings and one of them reported that all the men went to their deaths 'without the least sign of fear or dismay'. Afterwards their heads were impaled on poles and exhibited on St Mary's Bridge in Derby as a warning to other recusants. Their 'parts' were also displayed on the bridge until, in the night, they were taken away by 'two resolute Catholic gentlemen' who buried them secretly. A tablet in memory of these martyrs can be seen in St Mary's Roman Catholic Church, Derby.

John Fitzherbert's life was spared at a cost of £10,000 paid by his son-in-law but he was sent to the Fleet Prison to join his brother, Sir Thomas, who died there a few years later, and after ten years incarceration, John also died. His son, Anthony, was kept in the County gaol in Derby where he died of gaol fever.

The Padley estates were forfeited and the Manor House fell into ruins. Only the chapel survived. This simple gritstone building in the farmyard was frequently used as a cow byre or to house animal fodder. It also formed the gatehouse to the Manor, giving access to an inner courtyard. Here, foundations of the old Manor House can be traced and among them are a circular hearthstone, a stone oven and sink and two steps which are the beginning of a 14th century spiral staircase.

In 1933 the chapel was made use of as a shelter for navvies engaged in digging the Totley railway tunnel and many of the carved timbers it contained were burned or disfigured at that time.

Soon after this, however, work began on restoring the chapel and turning it into a memorial to the Padley martyrs. On July 13th 1933, for the first time in 345 years, mass was celebrated there. When the original altar stone, lost for centuries, was found under a mound of earth among the ruins, it was replaced in the chapel and used during services. The chapel now contains stained glass windows depicting its history and restoration. There are also windows in memory of the three priests who were put to death and to Sir Thomas and John Fitzherbert. In 1988 almost 1,000 children participated in the 400th anniversary service held on the site of the old Manor, a school band from Chesterfield supplying the music.

Pilgrimages to Padley take place annually. On the Thursday nearest to July 12th Roman Catholics from as far as Sheffield, Nottingham and Leeds assemble at Grindleford station. There they form a procession led by clergy which passes through a wood and crosses a stream before coming to the ruins of Padley Manor which is in the parish of Hathersage.

In the chapel a commemoration service is held and mass is celebrated in memory of the Padley martyrs whose cruel death was one of the many examples of the religious persecution that prevailed in England in the reign of Good Queen Bess.

The
Amazon of
Matlock Green

THE High Tor, a sheer limestone cliff, rises dramatically to 389 feet above the valley of the river Derwent at Matlock. On its eastern side are gentle slopes with fields and farms where once lived Phoebe Bown and her family.

Phoebe became a popular tourist attraction in Matlock at the end of the 18th century. Known as the 'Amazon of Matlock Green', she grew up developing what one writer called 'a dubious sex'. Another contemporary report described her as 'a well set-up female but with an unfortunate tendency to masculinity'. Her strength was recognised as truly remarkable for a girl for she could carry, with no apparent effort, a load of 2½ cwts. She was noted for taking part in 'fisticuffs' when she easily overcame any male contestant of her own age and size.

Phoebe was before her time in holding emphatic opinions on women's rights. She deplored the 18th century attitude to marriage and believed that the choosing of a wife at that time was no more than a business bargain. As she had very little money, Phoebe feared she would have no success in attracting a husband and, for this reason, she determined to become independent.

After her parents died, Phoebe lived alone on a small farm where she proved to be a successful cattle breeder. Capable of any kind of manual labour, she could guide a plough, drive a team of horses or thatch a barn and it was said that she became a competent carpenter, blacksmith and mason. A bold horse rider, she could 'ride or break a horse with the first jockey at Newmarket and had as keen a judgment of horseflesh as any horse dealer in the area'. Her favourite occupation was breaking in young horses for which she charged a guinea a week.

Visitors to Matlock would go to any lengths to catch a glimpse of this tall, strongly built figure dressed in a mixture of male and female attire. A petticoat and smock were worn beneath a man's woollen coat and, on her head were several handkerchiefs, knotted under her chin. These were topped by a man's high crowned hat.

When William Hutton, the historian, visited Matlock in 1802, he made a point of seeing Phoebe and left an account of his impressions of her. 'Her height is about five feet six inches', he wrote and, 'her step which is more manly than a man's can cover 40 miles a day'. He described her voice as 'more than masculine; with the wind in her favour, she can send it a mile'.

Phoebe was not uneducated and was familiar with the Classics, having been heard to quote at length from Shakespeare, Pope and Milton. She played, though not with great skill, several musical instruments and used the flute and cello in leading the choir at St Giles's church, Matlock. When a lady made her a present of a harpsichord, she built an extension to her cottage in which to contain it, though it was said she was never heard to play on it.

Visitors to her homestead were made welcome and she enjoyed discussing (and criticising) some of the families in the neighbourhood and also individuals she had read about. She was scornful of Lord Chesterfield's efforts to make his son a fine gentleman. 'Whitewash a red brick as much as you like,' she said, 'it is still a red brick and, at times, will show itself to be one.'

People well acquainted with Phoebe said that she enjoyed notoriety and, for this reason, she exploited her eccentricities. When a visitor from Liverpool suggested jokingly that Phoebe should pay her a visit, the lady was taken aback some time later in the middle of winter to find Phoebe on her doorstep. Disillusioned by the lady's inhospitable reception and embarrassed by the ridicule of her friends, Phoebe returned home to Matlock, on foot, having made the journey to Liverpool on horseback.

Full of superstition, Phoebe put her trust in omens and predictions but what presentiment caused her to harbour the fear of being robbed and murdered was never explained. The older she grew the more obsessed she became with the belief that neighbours and visitors alike were all conspiring to put her to death and steal her belongings. To guard against this eventuality, she filled her house with weapons so that it had the appearance of an armoury. Many of the swords, spears and bayonets found in every room she had manufactured herself and her cottage walls were covered with all types of guns.

In her old age Phoebe became unable to carry on with the farm work and found it impossible to make a living. Gradually, the tourists lost interest in her and so she became impoverished.

Fortunately, a relative of hers, Sarah Paxton who was the wife of Chatsworth's famous gardener, Joseph Paxton, approached the Duke of Devonshire on Phoebe's behalf and he made her an allowance of £13 a year for the rest of her life.

At her request, the Rev Gaunt, a curate at Matlock, wrote the following epitaph for her.

'Here lies romantic Phoebe,
Half Ganymede, half Hebe;
A maid of mutable condition,
A Jockey, Cowherd and Musician'.

It was said to 'please her mightily' but the verse was never inscribed on a tombstone, for Phoebe was buried with her brother's wife, Ann Bown. She died on May 16th 1854, aged about 85 years.

Faithful Tip

A STONE memorial to a dog stands by the western side of Howden reservoir in the High Peak district of Derbyshire. The monument was unveiled on April 30th 1955 in order to record the devotion of Tip, a collie bitch.

Owned by Joseph Tagg who lived at Bamford near the Yorkshire Bridge, Tip accompanied her master on numerous walks over the surrounding moorland. On 12th December 1953 they set off for a walk to the Howden moors and never returned.

The police were notified of Mr. Tagg's disappearance, search parties were arranged and, throughout the ensuing weeks of severe winter weather, the local moorland tracks were scoured for signs of the missing man and his dog, every possible route being followed that they might have taken.

On March 27th 1954, fifteen weeks after their disappearance, a local man named Samuel Bingham was walking on Howden moor when he thought he saw something move by the roadside. He walked over to the place to investigate and there he found the body of Mr. Tagg and, beside him in an emaciated condition, his faithful companion, Tip, keeping vigil over her master's corpse.

No-one knows how Tip survived for that length of time in such wintry conditions. She was taken to Mr. Tagg's niece, Mrs Thorp, who nursed her back to health and provided a comfortable home for the rest of her days.

At the Bamford Sheepdog Trials held on the following Whit Monday, Tip was presented with a bronze medal of the National Canine Defence League and a fund called 'A Tribute to Tip' was launched. The money raised was used to purchase a monument which was erected near the spot where she was found, close to her master's body, and it was there that Tip was buried when she died on February 16th 1955 shortly before the monument was unveiled.

Its inscription reads, 'In commemoration of the devotion of Tip, the sheepdog, which stayed by the body of her dead master, Mr. Joseph Tagg, on the Howden moors for fifteen weeks from the 12th December 1953 to 27th March 1954.'

Erected by public subscription.

The Royal Prisoner

WHEN Mary Queen of Scots set foot in Derbyshire for the first time, she was in a state of collapse. Having escaped from the Isle of Lochleven in Scotland where she was kept prisoner and made to sign a deed of abdication in favour of her son, the infant James, she determined to reach England and seek the protection of her 'good sister', Queen Elizabeth.

With her hair cropped and disguised as a peasant, she crossed the Solway Firth in a fishing boat but, disembarking on English soil, she found herself a prisoner once more. 'Use her honourably but do not allow her to escape', were Queen Elizabeth's instructions for she recognised the Scottish queen as a threat to her own security on the English throne. As a result she was placed in the custodianship of George Talbot, Earl of Shrewsbury, who had recently become the fourth husband of Bess of Hardwick.

Removed from Bolton Castle because she had already attempted an escape from there, the queen was forced to make the journey into Derbyshire during the wintry conditions of January 1569, travelling along roads which were no more than tracks of frozen slush. Accompanied by six ladies, a large number of servants and two companies of English troops, the

63

queen was not the only one suffering from cold and exhaustion on reaching Rotherham.

At Chesterfield, tormented by the pain in her side which recurred throughout her life, Queen Mary begged to be allowed to rest and the whole party found hospitality at Walton Hall, the home of Sir Godfrey Foljambe, and stayed there overnight.

After passing the next night at Wingfield Manor, one of Shrewsbury's houses, the cavalcade pressed on to Tutbury Castle, situated on the Derbyshire, Staffordshire border where the queen immediately took to her bed. Built after the Norman Conquest, the castle was partly in ruins and its rooms were damp, draughty and insanitary. Although Shrewsbury treated her with kindness and consideration and his wife did her best to make the royal prisoner comfortable, Queen Mary's health began to deteriorate. After many requests, Queen Elizabeth agreed to her being taken to Wingfield Manor where her apartments afforded delightful views over the village of Ashover.

But the queen remained seriously ill and two doctors, sent from London, admitted that her condition was aggravated by the insanitary conditions both inside and outside the manor. The Earl therefore arranged for the queen to be moved to Chatsworth, his wife's house, while a 'sweetening and cleansing' took place at Wingfield. Installed there once more when this had been completed, Queen Mary's main interest was her affectionate correspondence with Thomas Howard, Duke of Norfolk, whom she was now considering as a possible husband. A 33 year old Catholic widower, he was the richest landowner in the country. 'You have promised to be mine and I yours', she wrote. 'I believe the Queen of England and the country should like of it.'

When Shrewsbury had a slight stroke, Bess accompanied him to Buxton to take the waters and, while they were there, Queen Elizabeth heard of a plot that was being hatched by Leonard Dacre to help Queen Mary to escape from Wingfield and that the Duke of Norfolk was planning to marry her. In a fury she ordered the earl and his wife to return immediately and to transfer Queen Mary to Tutbury. The Duke of Norfolk was sent to the Tower.

When the plague became prevalent in the area Queen Mary was delighted to be moved to Chatsworth once more where her health improved and she rode daily.

Members of the Paget and Manners families visited her there to pay their respects and yet another scheme was devised for her escape. A group of local squires arranged to rescue her while she was out hunting but the plot came to nothing and the conspirators, Sir Thomas Gerard and Thomas and Edward Stanley, sons of the Earl of Derby, were betrayed by George Rolleston and spent two years in the Tower.

Now it was decided that the queen must be confined in a more strongly fortified prison. On a cold November morning in 1570, men working near Holmesfield watched a long line of riders climb over the hills from Baslow and cross the Totley moors. One of the retinue was Mary Queen of Scots who, weak and ill, had been obliged to mount her horse and undertake the rough journey of 15 miles to Sheffield Castle. Here, she became involved in another plot for her escape. An Italian Catholic named Ridolfi proposed to arrange an uprising in England to coincide with an invasion from the Netherlands, the aim being to capture Queen Elizabeth and place Queen Mary on the English throne with Norfolk, recently released from the Tower, as her consort.

Letters discovered in Queen Mary's writing left no doubt that she had sanctioned the undertaking. Norfolk, arrested together with some Derbyshire gentry including Francis Rolleston and his son from Ashbourne, was accused of high treason and condemned to death. Queen Mary, hearing this news, was 'all bewept and mourning'.

She was now more closely confined, the monotony of her existence relieved only by her accumulation of pets and in doing embroidery. Because of her frequent bouts of ill-health the beauty of her youth had disappeared by the time she was 40 yet, it was said, her 'alluring grace' never deserted her.

Queen Mary begged unceasingly to be allowed to visit Buxton and 'take the waters', famous for their healing properties. At length, when she was once more at Chatsworth, Queen Elizabeth gave her consent for Shrewsbury to 'carry her thither' in spite of the Earl's opinion that she made 'over much use of physic and baths'.

Shrewsbury's newly built house (on the site of the Old Hall Hotel) was described as 'a bewty to beholde with lodgings to the number of 30'. Here Queen Mary stayed for five weeks but was strictly supervised. All strangers were prevented from either entering or leaving the town while she was there and she was not allowed visitors after 9 pm.

Soon after her return to Chatsworth she was again moved to Sheffield and, from there, made two brief visits to Worksop Manor where she complained of her 'wretched little bedroom.'

She was allowed three more short breaks at Buxton but Queen Elizabeth became disturbed on account of the rumours that she was receiving visitors there. 'The Scottish queen doth mix too much', she protested and when the Earl of Leicester proposed to 'drink at Bukston's well', she ordered him to remain at Ashby and have the waters sent to him in a bottle.

On Queen Mary's last visit to the spa in 1584, she wrote with a diamond on the window of her bedroom,

'Buxton, whose fame thy milk-warm waters tell,

Whom I, perchance, no more shall see, farewell.'

Soon afterwards she was put in the charge of Sir Ralph Sadler who was ordered to keep her at Wingfield Manor where 210 men were employed in the business of her custody and 8 gentlemen were on duty outside her bedroom each night. At the beginning of 1585, however, in spite of her many tearful protests, she was taken back to Tutbury on Queen Elizabeth's orders.

'The wayes being so foule and deepe', she had to spend a night in Derby on the way. Here all the streets were cleared for the arrival of the queen and her retinue. Her coach 'groaned' over St Mary's Bridge and stopped at Babington

House, owned by the Babington family of Dethick. 'Having no husbands to trouble us, we should get on well together,' remarked the queen to her hostess, Mrs. Beaumont.

The custodianship of the Scottish queen placed an enormous strain on both Shrewsbury's time and his resources and his marriage suffered as a result. His wife, family and servants were all resentful about their lack of freedom while the queen was in his care.

When Queen Mary discovered that Bess had plans for her granddaughter, Arbella Stuart, to become Queen of England she wrote furiously to Queen Elizabeth exposing the treacherous tales Bess had told about Elizabeth and the Earl of Leicester. Shocked by his wife's behaviour, Shrewsbury begged to be relieved of his post as Queen Mary's gaoler and he and Bess separated for good. The earl thanked Queen Elizabeth for thus setting him free of two devils, his wife and the Queen of Scots.

At Tutbury, Queen Mary was handed over to the care of Sir Amyas Paulet, a severe man and a zealous Puritan.

After several other conspiracies involving her, culminating in the Babington plot, Queen Mary was taken to Fotheringay where she was tried and found guilty of 'conspiring against the reigning monarch'. But Queen Elizabeth delayed pronouncing the death sentence until February 1587 when the execution took place. On hearing the news of Queen Mary's death, she 'shed an abundance of tears'.

Shrovetide Traditions

THE Pancake Bell used to be rung on Shrove Tuesday morning in every town and village throughout Derbyshire. Now, except in a few places like Chapel-en-le-Frith and Castleton, the custom has lapsed.

Originally, this bell had nothing to do with pancakes. It was the Shriving Bell that summoned people to church to confess their sins. This was in preparation for the abstinence of Lent which followed and lasted 40 days and 40 nights. During this time people ate only plain food, forgoing any 'flesh of quadruped, fowl or fish', thus following the example of Christ who fasted for 40 days and nights before his crucifixion. Anyone enjoying a good meal in Lent could expect to be excluded from the Resurrection.

On Shrove Tuesday supplies of butter and fats that could not be preserved were used up in pancakes, known in the Middle Ages as 'fritters'.

According to a legend, a Derbyshire woman in the 15th century heard the Shrovetide bell while she was cooking pancakes and rushed to church still holding the frying pan in her hand. This incident is recalled at Winster, an ancient market town near Matlock. Here, on Shrove Tuesday, competitors of all ages run races between the Dower House and the Market Place carrying a pancake in a frying pan.

Eventually the Shrovetide bell came to be recognised as a

signal for housewives to mix the batter for their pancakes, children singing as they stirred in turn,

'Mix a pancake, stir a pancake,
Pop it in the pan,
Fry the pancake, toss the pancake,
Catch it if you can.'

In Derbyshire schools the children delighted in carrying on the traditional 'barring out' of the schoolmaster and this custom continued until the Second World War. Having barricaded themselves in their classrooms, they chanted, when the teacher arrived,

'Pardon, Mister, pardon,
Pardon in a spoon,
If you don't give us a holiday,
We'll bar you out till noon.'

If the teacher managed to force an entry the children could expect to be chastised but they were usually granted a holiday in the afternoon and this was spent in playing with whips and tops or battle-dores and shuttlecocks. Older pupils would roam round the village begging pancakes, eggs and cheese and saying,

'Here I come, I never came before,
If you don't give me a pancake,
I'll break down your door.'

At the doors of houses where they were not given anything, they threw stones and broken crockery.

The most popular Shrovetide game was communal football, known as 'Hug Ball' because the ball was not allowed to touch the ground nor rise in the air, and described as 'a wild riot with no proper teams or fixed rules'.

When the barbaric natives of Derby, then called Derventio, succeeded in driving out the Roman legionnaires from the town, they celebrated with a game of football, originally using a human skull instead of a ball. It was traditionally played by men on Shrove Tuesday and boys on Ash Wednesday, the latter being the day on which many free fights took place. Each day the bells of five churches rang out.

'Pancakes and fritters say All Saints and Saint Peter's,
When will the ball come? say the bells of Saint Alkmund.
At two they will throw, says Saint Werebo (St Werburgh).
Oh, very well, says little Michel.'

The streets were thronged with players and onlookers and
the ball was thrown by the mayor from a window of the
Guildhall at noon. The two goals were at opposite ends of the
town, parishioners of All Saints aiming for Gallows Bank on
the Normanton Road while those belonging to Saint Peter's
parish attacked the goal at Nun's Mill.

On one occasion the number of males taking part in the game
was estimated at over 1,000 and, according to one report,
players were 'not confined to the lower classes alone; the gentry
and respectable people joined in'.

When the ball fell into the Markeaton Brook which carried
it into the River Derwent, the struggles in the water often
proved dangerous and, in 1797 a man taking part was drowned.
At the inquest, the jury condemned the contest as a 'disgrace
to humanity and civilisation'. After a number of serious
casualties had occurred every year, the game was finally banned
in 1848 when a notice on the Town Hall read, 'Any person
found in the public streets or passages or other public places
within this borough for the purpose of playing football will be
prosecuted'. Before law and order could be established,
however, special constables were hastily appointed, two troops
of dragoons were brought into the town and the Riot Act was
read in the Market Place.

By 1821, the Shrovetide game was well established in
Ashbourne when the Shrovetide Ballad was composed and sung
in the old Ashbourne theatre.

'Shrove Tuesday, you know, is always the day
When pancake's the prelude and football's the play,
Where Uppards and Down'ards men, ready for fun,
Like French at the Battle of Waterloo run.'

The Uppards are those born north of the Henmore Brook
which divides the town and the Down'ards are those born to

71

the south of it. A celebrity is invited to 'turn up' the ball which is made in Ashbourne and stuffed with cork shavings, and he is traditionally entertained to lunch at the 'Green Man'. In 1928 the Prince of Wales, later the Duke of Windsor, opened the game which was, thereafter, called Royal Football.

Played from 2 pm until midnight on Shrove Tuesday, the game continues on Ash Wednesday. Windows of houses and shops are all boarded up first thing in the morning for no compensation can be claimed for damage to property. It has developed into a desperately rough game and a Frenchman passing through Ashbourne one Shrove Tuesday remarked, 'If this is the way the English play, what are they like when they are fighting?'

Two old mills, three miles apart, used to act as goals but, when these were demolished, posts on the same site were erected for the purpose. It is mutually understood that the churchyard, the cemetery, the War Memorial and the Recreation Ground are out of bounds.

Inevitably the ball lands in the Henmore brook and the struggle for its possession continues in the water. Whoever scores a goal is allowed to keep the ball and a new one is brought into play. More than two goals a day have never been recorded and one year a goal was scored by a young woman named Mrs Mugglestone.

At the end of the 19th century determined attempts were made to stamp out the game and every Shrove Tuesday the police were ordered to keep a sharp lookout for the ball. On one occasion it was secretly passed to a Mrs Woolley while she was out shopping on Shrove Tuesday morning. Hiding it under her skirts, she took it home and, later in the day, threw it from her bedroom window into the Market Place when the game immediately began.

The magistrates imposed many fines but all were paid by public subscription and so the game has been allowed to continue indefinitely.

A Spinner
of Tales

HIGH on a hill at Cromford near Matlock stands Castle Top Farm. An Elizabethan house, it overlooks the valley of the River Derwent, known to locals as the 'Darrand'.

In December 1884 Derbyshire lay under a succession of heavy falls of snow, blocking country roads and isolating villages. The steep track leading to Castle Top Farm was banked with snowdrifts making it impossible to get the churns of milk down to Cromford station.

Henry Taylor worked from morning till night, digging his way to the cow sheds and, with snow up to his armpits, attempting to cut his way to rescue sheep buried on the hillsides.

Owned by the Arkwrights of Willersley Castle at Cromford who used it as a base for shooting parties, the farm had been tenanted by the Taylor family for three generations.

Henry's second wife was Hannah Dickenson and at this time when snow enveloped the farm, she was expecting her first baby. It was fortunate that a midwife had managed to get through while the roads were negotiable and, on December 17th, Alice Jane was born who, in later years, became the famous writer of stories, Alison Uttley.

In her books she describes her early life on the farm when small children were expected to make themselves useful, opening gates for the cows at milking time, holding their tails to prevent them lashing the faces of the milkers and feeding the cade lambs whose mothers had died and had to be bottle fed in the farmhouse kitchen.

Here was a big open range from which the firelight was reflected in the brass candlesticks, warming pans and dish covers and the guns hanging on the walls. There was a grandfather clock which had stopped when Alison's grandfather died and did not start ticking again until after he was buried. At two separate tables, the family and servants, indoor and outdoor, had their own places at mealtimes.

Various 'visitors' were welcomed at different times of the year. Mr Moldy Warp came with his traps for catching moles, the rat catcher arrived with his bag of ferrets and the old pedlar, puffing up the hill with his load of pans and kettles, took payment in rabbit skins. When the pig sticker appeared, Alison ran indoors with her fingers in her ears to shut out the squeals.

At haymaking time a party of Irishmen came to help with the harvest. They slept in one of the barns and, leaning from her bedroom window, Alison listened to them talking as they sat outside in the dusk, smoking their pipes. It was a language she was unable to understand.

On Christmas Eve, Alison and the servant girl joined in the singing of carol singers who stood outside with their lanterns and afterwards were offered Mrs Taylor's elderberry wine and mince pies in the parlour.

Every Sunday, Alison went to church with her mother. Her father could never be persuaded to go. In *The Country Child* she describes their hurried departure carrying prayer books, threepenny bits for collection and lozenges to suck during the long, long sermon. Peeping over the edge of the pew, she could see the Arkwright ladies in their beaded bonnets and silken gowns and the squire who was brave enough to turn round during the service.

Not being allowed to play games on Sundays, Alison used old envelopes on which to write little stories and poems about the wild creatures who lived in the fields and woods surrounding the farm.

74

Alison was taught to read and write by her mother and she, in turn, taught the servant girl but, at the age of seven, she had to embark on the daily four mile walk to school. This took her through the frightening Bow Wood which was so dark and creepy that she carried a storm lantern with a candle inside to light the way.

The beginning of Alison's schooldays was an unhappy period when she was jeered at because of her old fashioned clothes and taunted when, at the end of the afternoon, she fell asleep at her desk. As an excuse to stay at home, she often invented a sore throat or earache and sometimes she played truant, hiding all day in one of the barns. Frequently caned for inattention, she found that this raised her standing with the other pupils and, at last, she began to make friends. Her abiding love of music was inspired and fostered by the schoolmaster, Mr. Allen.

When Alison's godmother sent her an Easter egg, she invited every girl in the school to go home with her and inspect it. Dumbfounded, Mrs Taylor watched the excited swarm of children emerge from the wood but, after a few moments, she rose to the occasion and hurried to find food for them all. Newly baked bread, cakes and pastries intended for the family's and servants' meals during the week were soon devoured eagerly by the children as they sat on the farmyard wall.

'Are you clean daft crazy to bring all those cackling childer here?' demanded her father after the last of them had departed. But Alison was upset only because she had forgotten to show them her Easter egg.

Sometimes Alison and her brother rode in the milk cart taking the churns to the station and, occasionally, they accompanied their father on his weekly trip to Cromford village where he bought flour from the mill and cattle medicine from the druggist. The children stood by the forge watching the blacksmith hammering a horseshoe on his anvil or pressed their noses to the window of the General Stores in order to decide what to buy with their Saturday penny. Outings to the wakes held in the yard of the 'Greyhound' were special treats and once a year the family visited relatives at Carsington, driving through the Via Gellia which Alison called 'the loveliest valley in the world'.

After winning a County Minor Scholarship, Alison became a pupil at the Lady Manners School at Bakewell. In *Carts and Candlesticks* she describes her daily ride in the milk cart to Cromford station followed by the train journey to Bakewell in which boys and girls had to occupy separate compartments. It did not take long for her to discover that being a scholarship holder had its disadvantages for the fee payers thought themselves superior and were discouraged by the staff from sharing a hymn book with the 'Poor free education' students. Alison's propensity for imaginative writing was firmly squashed by an English master who read aloud the children's essays and ridiculed their efforts.

In spite of these drawbacks, Alison distinguished herself at the end of six years by winning a County Major Scholarship and gaining a place to read for a degree in physics and chemistry at Manchester University where she found herself the only female in that faculty.

By this time Alison realised that she possessed mystical powers. She had premonitions and often read accounts in the newspapers of events she had dreamed about the night before. In a trance like state, she would sometimes experience occurrences which had taken place centuries before. As a result of one of these incidents, she wrote *A Traveller in Time* in which the Babington plot and the execution of Mary Queen of Scots were interwoven with the life of a Derbyshire girl in the 19th century.

After taking her degree, Alison trained as a teacher in Cambridge and then obtained a post in Fulham, south west London.

In 1911 she married James Uttley, a civil engineer, and they settled at Knutsford in Cheshire. When her husband died, she took up writing seriously in order to provide for her son's education and this was the beginning of the 'Little Grey Rabbit' series of children's books. The first of her autobiographical books, *The Country Child*, was soon published and followed by more and more stages of her childhood at Castle Top Farm.

In 1936 Alison moved to Buckinghamshire where she lived in a cottage called 'Thackers', filled with furniture from her old home at Cromford, including the grandfather clock.

Becoming somewhat eccentric in her old age, Alison continued to live alone with her Scottie dog, Macduff. Local people recognised her as 'the old lady who ties up her hair with a coloured ribbon'. She died on May 5th 1976, aged ninety-one, and was buried at Penn, near Beaconsfield. Her simple headstone bears the words,

'Alison Uttley, a Spinner of Tales.'

The
Pentrich Revolt

T HE quiet little village of Pentrich lies between South Wingfield and Ripley, situated along the side of one of the last hills belonging to the Pennine Chain. In June 1817 its name made national headlines but the Parish Register recorded succinctly, 'On the evening of 9th June an Insurrection broke out in Pentrich, South Wingfield, Swanwick and Ripley which was quelled next day at, or in the region of, Kimberley'.

When the Napoleonic Wars came to an end in 1815, thousands of men from all parts of the country were released from the forces causing a sharp rise in unemployment. Wages fell, prices rose and crime increased. Discontent became widespread as many families were living in poverty with children always hungry. In the Pentrich area, stockingers were taken into the workhouse by the dozen.

As a result, seditious societies sprang up, a large number in the Midlands hosiery towns. One popular meeting place was in Pentrich at the White Horse Inn and it was here that Jeremiah Brandreth, a 27 year old framework knitter from Sutton-in-Ashfield, but thought to be an Exeter man, recruited a band of local weavers, stockingers and labourers and outlined his plans to march to Nottingham where they were expected to join thousands of men from other counties. Their aim was to proceed, altogether, to London and overthrow Lord Liverpool's unpopular government.

The instigator of this insurrection was believed to be Oliver, an 'agent provocateur' for the government, who incited Brandreth to lead the revolt, calling him the 'Nottingham Captain'.

On June 9th about 400 men and boys, referred to later as 'those poor misguided villagers', set out for Nottingham, many of those living in Pentrich having gone to pray at the parish church on the previous night. Brandreth's plan was to raid farms on the way in order to take possession of what shot guns and other weapons they could lay their hands on. He also intended to take over the works at Butterley, collecting men and arms for the use of his army.

An unfortunate incident when Brandreth shot and killed a manservant at Mrs Hepworth's farm in Wingfield Park had a sobering effect on the whole company. Mrs Hepworth was a widow whose son, Francis, managed the farm. He had refused to take part in the revolt and, hearing that an attempt would be made on his life as a result, he allowed his mother to persuade him to leave the village for a time.

When the insurrectionists were heard knocking on the farmhouse door, Mrs Hepworth was in the house together with her two daughters and a son, William, and two manservants. As she refused to admit anyone from outside, Brandreth forced open a window at the back of the house and fired a shot that struck Robert Walters, one of the servants, as he was lacing his boots. He was killed on the spot and when some of the men remonstrated with Brandreth he threatened to kill them as well.

After collecting all the weapons in the house, the party left but requisitioned more arms from several houses in the neighbourhood before advancing to Butterley. More men were enlisted on the way, Brandreth's method of recruitment being to force them out of bed and make them get dressed at gun point, threatening to blow out their brains if they refused to join his army.

At the Butterley Iron Works, Brandreth had expected to meet some resistance from the employees but, as they arrived there in the pouring rain, they found only Mr. Goodwin, one of the managers, awaiting them and he immediately upbraided them for embarking on such a foolhardy expedition. They were all putting halters round their necks, he warned them, and would certainly get hanged.

Confronted by this attitude, Brandreth, to the astonishment of his followers, appeared to be totally taken aback and made no reply. After some hesitation, he gave the command to 'march' but not before Mr. Goodwin had recognised some of the younger men and pushed them into his office, forbidding them to continue with the Captain's reckless undertaking.

It was said that, because of Brandreth's strong personality, his commanding presence with black flashing eyes and a big black beard, and his plausible promises of a better life after their victory, very few of his recruits, once having joined, would wish to forsake his leadership. But the Captain's uncharacteristic wavering at Butterley produced in his followers a feeling of mistrust and uncertainty and, as they marched off to Ripley, many looked for an opportunity to make' their escape.

However, Brandreth and his leaders, including Ludlam, Weightman and Turner, did their best to raise the men's flagging spirits and at Codnor a halt was made to supply the army with food and drink. Some went to the Glasshouse Inn, some to the New Inn and some to the French Horn where refreshment was provided, Brandreth promising payment when they had achieved their object.

Now the numbers were augmented by a large party of men from Swanwick but the men's morale was still at a low ebb and many disturbances occurred, settled by the Captain's customary threat to blow their brains out. Arriving at Langley Mill, they found everyone talking of the news received in the town that soldiers from Nottingham were on their way to encounter the insurrectionists. At this, the whole army began to disperse, going in all directions and ignoring the Captain's orders to fall in line again. Having been tipped off by Oliver, a detachment of the 15th Hussars stationed in readiness at Nottingham was already on its way in pursuit of Brandreth's army. What was left of it they discovered at Giltbrook, a village between Kimberley and Eastwood. In a state of panic on seeing the red coats, the men threw down their arms and ran. The disorganised rabble of an army was then hunted down by the soldiers and some 40 of them were captured. Three to four dozen guns and pikes were collected which had been discarded by the roadsides.

The men who escaped fled back to Pentrich and hid for days in ditches and haystacks, in local barns and in the graveyard.

The prisoners were held in Derby and Nottingham gaols until October 15th when their trials began at the County Hall, this having been enlarged for the occasion.

At the end of September Mr. Thomas Hallowes, the High Sheriff of the county arrived in Derby accompanied by numerous attendants and, soon afterwards, two judges from London entered the town. Two hundred men had been summoned as special constables and three hundred jurymen were called, the latter including Lord George Augustus Cavendish, as foreman, the Hon. George Vernon and Sir Robert Wilmot. To these were added 268 witnesses for the prosecution and an undefined number for the defence. As can be imagined, the town was also thronged with onlookers, 'under', one newspaper reported, 'the mere impulse of curiosity'.

The proceedings lasted for ten days. As the ringleaders, Brandreth, Ludlam, Turner and Weightman were brought into court, the clanking of the irons on their legs resounded through the courtroom, causing a profound silence. Some said that Oliver ought to have been in the dock, alongside them. The indictment stated that the prisoners, 'being moved and seduced by the Devil, did maliciously and traitorously attempt, by force and arms, to destroy the Government and Constitution of the realm'.

Placing the black cap on his head, the Lord Chief Justice pronounced the sentence. – 'You are to be drawn on a hurdle,' he stated, 'to the place of your execution and there be severally hanged until you are dead; your heads must then be severed from your bodies.' Weightman's sentence was, at a later date, commuted to transportation in the company of fourteen others. The rest of the insurrectionists were pardoned.

Taken back to their cells, the prisoners spent much time in prayer although Brandreth appeared to be quite composed and was frequently seen in the prison yard smoking his pipe. The men all received visits from their wives and families which occasioned some distressing scenes. Brandreth's wife made the journey on foot from Sutton in Ashfield but he refused to have any communication made with his parents. Many touching letters were preserved, sent by the prisoners during the time before their execution which took place on November 7th. The number of spectators on that occasion was estimated at over 6,000.

When the victims' heads were held up to face the crowd, many women fainted and some hastened quickly away from the gruesome spectacle. The corpses were buried in a communal grave at St Werburgh's church in Derby. The block used for their execution can be seen in the Derby Museum.

'May the Ground Swallow Me Up'

THE tall spire of All Saints' Church, Ashover, is a familiar landmark in the beautiful Amber valley. The church contains the oldest lead font in the county, made about 1150, and the third of its peal of bells bears the inscription, 'The old bell rung the fall of Bonaparte and broke, April 1814'.

In the Parish Register it is recorded, '1660 Dorothy Mately, supposed wife of Jno Flint of this parish, foreswore herself, whereupon the ground opened and she sanke over hed Mar. 23rd, and being found dead, she was buried Mar. 25th'.

Dorothy Mately had a reputation for swearing, cursing, lying and thieving and became so notorious that the contemporary writer, John Bunyan, compared her to his 'Mr. Badman'. Whenever she protested her innocence in any accusation made against her, she would say, 'I would that I might sink into the earth', or 'I would God make the earth open and swallow me up if this be so'.

Dorothy was employed along with other local women and some boys on the surface of a lead mine about a quarter of a mile from the village centre. Every day they washed away the 'spoil' from the ore as it was brought up from the mine.

On this particular day, a boy who had taken off his breeches and laid them aside and was working in his 'drawers' found that two pennies were missing from his breeches pocket. Well aware of Dorothy's character, he accused her of stealing them.

Hotly, she denied having done such a thing and wished the ground would swallow her up if she had taken them.

George Hodgkinson, an Ashover man, was standing nearby as Dorothy was swearing her innocence but he took the hand of a little girl who was standing beside him and drew her away as someone was calling her. Before they had gone ten yards, however, they heard Dorothy screaming for help and, turning round, they saw her spin round and round before disappearing into the ground together with the work tub.

Having sunk about three yards, she came to rest and again began to yell for help but, just as Mr. Hodgkinson was about to go towards the hole into which she had fallen, a large stone from the side fell on her head, breaking her skull. Immediately more earth fell over her and around her, covering her completely.

She was eventually dug out being found four yards below the surface but her tub never came to light although the boy's two pennies were found in her pocket.

Being a lead mining area, the ground would be full of shafts and likely to collapse at any time but most people believed that Dorothy's tragic end came as a suitable retribution for her behaviour.

The Custom of Well Dressing

THE rural custom of 'dressing' wells by means of pictures made of flowers is unique to Derbyshire.

The early villages of the county were situated in the Mountain Limestone areas of the Peak District where wells and springs abound. Their pagan inhabitants made sacrifices to water gods in thanksgiving for a perpetual supply of water and a plea for its continuation. Later, they abandoned the cruel destruction of human and animal life and substituted flowers which were thrown into the wells or hung in garlands over the springs.

The first well dressing ceremony in the county to be recorded took place at Tissington on Ascension Day in 1350, following the worst epidemic of the Bubonic Plague ever experienced in Europe. When this scourge, called the Black Death, wiped out half the population of Derbyshire and 77 out of 100 clergy in the county perished, only one person in the village of Tissington died. This was attributed to the purity of the water supply from the local wells.

In 1615 England suffered the worst drought in history. The parish register in Youlgreave church recalls, 'There was no rayne fell upon ye earth from the 25th daye of March to the 2nd of May and then there was but one shower. Two more fell betweene then and the 4th daye of August so that the greatest part of the land was burnt up bothe corne and haye.' Yet the wells at Tissington never ran dry and people flocked from miles around to obtain water for themselves and their animals.

The latter event would certainly revive the ancient custom of well-dressing if ever it had been allowed to lapse and, since that time, the five wells at Tissington and latterly a sixth, dressed entirely by children, have been decorated annually on Ascension Day, also known as Holy Thursday.

Situated a few miles north of Ashbourne, Tissington is, indisputably, the prettiest village in Derbyshire. An almost perfectly preserved estate village with the Hall in the centre, it has been the home of the Fitzherbert family for nearly four hundred years.

As the 'mother-place' of well-dressing, it attracts much publicity and numerous visitors at Ascensiontide when crowds watch the ceremony of 'Blessing the Wells' and join in the accompanying service.

With the arrival of piped water, some villages began to decorate their taps and standpipes in a similar way, Wirksworth being one of the first to celebrate the installation of a water supply by 'tap-dressings' in 1827. At present the dressing of nine wells or taps (or, in some cases, the sites where these taps used to be) in this village takes place on the Saturday before Spring Bank Holiday. There is keen competition among the dressers here as a silver cup is given for first place. On the same date, three wells are dressed in Derby, two of them being of Roman origin and only recently discovered. The third is St. Alkmund's Well by which the saint's coffin rested while a church to his memory was built nearby. Its water was believed to have health giving properties, 'many screaming babies being dipped therein'.

Among the first wells to be dressed when flowers become available are the eight at Etwall which are decorated in mid-May. Situated in the south of the county, the village has a greater choice of earlier flowers than could be found further north at this time of the year.

From village to village there are differences in the structure of the wooden framework on which the pictures are made and in the types of flowers used. Called 'screens', the frames are first soaked in water (at Tissington in the village pond) and then covered in clay. The clay is 'puddled' with water and salt before being applied to the screens, the salt keeping the clay moist, thus preserving the flowers, and preventing cracks caused by the heat of the sun.

Creating the flower pictures is a craft handed down from one generation to another. Men and women of all ages take part, including older people who have done the work for many years and children who are encouraged to give a helping hand in order to provide the next generation of dressers.

The picture is drawn, full size, on paper and this is placed over the clay foundation. The design is pricked out by means of some sharp instrument and then the paper is peeled away, leaving the outlines. These are made clearer by pressing into them berries, tiny alder cones and sometimes little haricot beans. Everything used in the process is of natural origin, human hair and sheep's wool being acceptable and sometimes even coal. Bark, mosses and lichen are found useful for the background effects and then begins the 'flowering' when, in some pictures, only petals are used, each being pressed into the clay individually.

Roughly, three out of every four pictures illustrate a bible scene with a text or a caption added, also worked in flowers. The completed picture on the screen, which is sometimes the size of a large door, is pulled to the well by a tractor and positioned securely over or behind it.

There are now more than 30 Derbyshire villages in which wells, springs or taps are dressed annually. Some play a part in the celebration of a holy day such as Whit Sunday or the date is chosen in recognition of the church's patronal festival. Others celebrate the anniversary of some important event like the centenary of the village school at Litton or the erection of a memorial to some well-known resident.

Elsewhere, well-dressings often coincide with the local wakes week when carnival activities take place. Houses, shops and streets are decorated and processions, accompanied by brass bands and headed by the Carnival King and Queen, attract throngs of spectators.

Well dressings in June include five at Youlgreave on the nearest Sunday to John the Baptist's day, June 24th. These celebrate the bringing of water from a spring outside the village to a newly built reservoir known as 'The Fountain' in 1829. On the same day, Tideswell's four wells are decorated. The ebbing and flowing well in the village was one of the Seven Wonders of the Peak.

On the last Saturday in June Bakewell's five wells are dressed. Rood Well is commonly called 'Eye Well' as its waters were thought to contain properties for curing eye troubles. On the Saturday nearest to St. Peter's Day, June 29th, three wells are dressed at Hope where cultivated flowers are preferred to wild ones.

Buxton's three wells are dressed early in July. St. Anne's well was a healing spring in medieval times, its 'milk-warm' waters being enjoyed by Mary Queen of Scots on her six visits there while she was a prisoner in Derbyshire. It was said to maintain a temperature of 82 degrees Fahrenheit and the sticks and crutches abandoned there bear witness to its curative powers. This well was first dressed to commemorate the introduction of piped water to the town by the Duke of Devonshire in the mid 19th century.

In the small square called 'The Nook' at Stoney Middleton two wells are decorated in the last week in July. Behind the church is a warm spring that once had a bath house next to it.

On the Wednesday following St. Lawrence's Day, August 10th, three wells are dressed at Barlow where whole flowers are used instead of petals. For the well at Eyam, now called Mompesson's Well, late summer flowers and autumn leaves are used on the last Saturday in August. At the end of this month thousands of visitors make a pilgrimage to Wormhill, high in the Peak, where the well erected to James Brindley, the notable canal engineer, more than 100 years after his death, is dressed on the Saturday before the late Summer Bank Holiday.

Near most wells collecting boxes are placed, unobtrusively, and from these, donations are made to both national and local charities, thus benefiting everyone.

George Curzon: Viceroy

THE Curzons came to England with William the Conqueror and have, without interruption, occupied Kedleston Hall in South Derbyshire for more than 800 years. In 1198-9 the inheritance, including lands at Croxall and Kedleston under the de Ferrers, was divided between two sons. Thomas de Curzon took Kedleston for his share and from him is descended the present family.

There are no remains of earlier buildings preceding the impressive Georgian mansion which was built between the years 1759 and 1770 when the title of its owner had changed to Nathaniel, 1st Baron Scarsdale.

Alfred, the 4th Baron Scarsdale, was a clergyman, rector of Kedleston and Mickleover. Neither he nor his wife devoted much time to their children and spared them little love or affection. In spite of the prosperity of the estate, the family lived quite frugally and George, the eldest son and heir born in 1859, spent most of his childhood days in the company of servants with the result that, all his life, he retained a broad Derbyshire accent.

At Eton he was rarely visited by either of his parents and felt himself rejected. One of his poignant letters home ends, 'I was sorry I was all alone and everybody else's people came. Your loving boy, George.'

A brilliant scholar at Oxford, he won every major prize at

Balliol College and has been called 'the most academically distinguished Oxonian of all time'. Aged 26, he became MP for Southport and, in 1891, Under Secretary of State for India.

Compared to his social class contemporaries, George Curzon was a poor man but in 1895 he married an heiress. Mary Leiter was the beautiful daughter of Levi Leiter, an American millionaire who, on the marriage settled a million dollars on Mary and £6,000 a year on the couple jointly, promising in addition a similar sum to each child of the union.

The marriage took place at Easter 1895 in Washington and was a brilliant society event. Soon afterwards the bridal couple sailed for England and, after an uncomfortable voyage, travelled straight to Derbyshire. The streets of Derby were decorated and church bells rang out in welcome as 35,000 people lined the road from Derby station to Kedleston when George Curzon brought his bride to his ancestral home. There she met her husband's parents, his three brothers, six sisters and 550 tenants.

In June, Curzon was appointed Under Secretary of State for Foreign Affairs and in July Mary helped him in canvassing in his Southport constituency.

'I loathe this miserable seaside resort', Mary wrote to her parents but his opponents declared that her husband owed his success 'far more to the winning smiles of his American wife than to his own speeches'.

On their return to Kedleston, Mary became critical of her father-in-law, calling him 'the most tyrannical old man I have ever seen'. She pitied his spinster daughters whom he reproached for not being married yet never allowed to meet any suitable men. 'An old despot of the 13th century', she described him to her parents.

Mary continued to find fault with the climate in Derbyshire, her husband's family and the servants at Kedleston but, in 1898 when she was expecting her second child, the life of the Curzons changed dramatically. On Queen Victoria's recommendation,

George was appointed Viceroy of India and was created Baron Curzon of Kedleston.

'Oh, the ladyships,' wrote Mary. 'I feel like a ship in full sail on the high seas of dignity'.

They were given the freedom of the city of London, attended a ball at Buckingham Palace and were 'treated like grandees'.

Before sailing to India they were invited to Windsor when the queen presented Mary with jewels and congratulated Curzon on his wife's beauty.

The voyage took three weeks and they arrived in Bombay on December 30th. After entering Calcutta under a gold umbrella (ancient symbol of Indian royalty), Mary wrote to her parents, 'We might as well be monarchs'.

Government House with its enormous rooms had been modelled on Kedleston Hall. Curzon attempted to modernise the building but it was years before a single bathroom with running water was installed.

It was said that Curzon added to his term of office in India 'a glitter and dignity' and he dedicated himself wholeheartedly to the Raj. He undertook important administrative changes including the partition of Bengal and restored many fine Indian buildings, such as the Taj Mahal, to their original splendour.

Mary enjoyed the pomp and ceremony. Tall and slim, she wore the most wonderful clothes and jewels, notably the famous 'peacock dress' in which, as Vicereine, she presided at the Coronation Durbar, held to acclaim King Edward VII as Emperor of India. This was in 1903 and, the following year, she sailed to England for the birth of her third child, another daughter.

Soon after the baby was born, Mary became seriously ill and Curzon, having hurried back from India, spent hours at her bedside. She gave him instructions about her funeral and said farewell to the children but, surprisingly, she recovered and Curzon returned for his second term of office in India.

In February Mary embarked at Tilbury to join him, accompanied by the three little girls, two nurses and a live cow in the hold to supply fresh milk for the baby. A thousand people gave her an enthusiastic welcome at Government House and her health soon appeared to be completely restored.

The Vicereine's health was, once more, giving cause for concern and, later in the year, the family returned to England.

'I fear I shall never be well again', wrote Mary. She grew gradually worse and died suddenly of a heart attack at the age of thirty six. According to her wishes, she was buried at Kedleston and tributes at the funeral came from King Edward and Queen Alexandra and from the President of the USA. 'Mourned in three continents,' Curzon wrote, 'she left me with three motherless children and a broken life.'

Before long, he was appointed Lord Warden of the Cinque Ports and Chancellor of Oxford University. He renewed his acquaintance with Elinor Glyn, the novelist, and carried on an affair with her until, after some years, he met and married Grace, the rich widow of Alfred Duggan, the American writer.

Gaining political power once more, Curzon became Lord Privy Seal and a member of the War Cabinet. Feeling certain of being made Prime Minister when Bonar Law resigned in 1923, he was bitterly humiliated to learn that Baldwin had been chosen instead. A suggested reason for Curzon's failure to secure the Premiership was that, in 1921, he had been created Marquess of Kedleston and had, thus, 'lost the common touch', an impression fostered by the popular contemporary rhyme,

'George Nathaniel Curzon,

A most superior person'.

The Marquess did not succeed his father until 1916 so his plans for modernising Kedleston were not carried out before he died in 1925. He was buried in the Curzon chapel adjoining Kedleston church which he had built in memory of his wife, Mary, 'perfect in love and loveliness'. Their effigies in marble lie there, side by side, her hand clasped in his.

No Whistling
in the Mine

IT has been estimated that there are between 50,000 and
100,000 old mine shafts in Derbyshire, many of them still
uncapped and dangerous to unsuspecting walkers. They are
memorials to the lead mining industry which was carried on
in Britain from pre-Roman times until the middle of the present
century.

Before the Roman occupation, lead ore was obtained in the
north Pennines so it is supposed that veins in the Derbyshire
Peak district were also worked at that time. Extraction of lead
by the Romans was mainly from open workings or outcrops
where the lead was found not far from the surface.

Several crude ingots or 'pigs' of lead unearthed from time
to time in the last two centuries have furnished no reliable
information as to where exactly they were mined. One of these
came to light quite near the surface at Cromford in 1777.
Weighing 126 lbs, it bears an inscription in Latin denoting that
it belonged to the Emperor Hadrian. Since then, others have
been found at Matlock Bank, Tansley Moor and Bradwell and
some bear the letters LVT which is believed to refer to
Lutudarum, an area between Wirksworth and Matlock or
possibly around Chesterfield.

After the Romans withdrew, lead mining continued in the
county, albeit on a smaller scale, by the Saxons and Danes.
Odin Mine on the Mam Tor road is believed to have been
worked by the latter.

In the 9th century there were mines at Wirksworth owned by the Abbey of Repton which paid an annual rent of lead worth 300 shillings to Christ Church, Canterbury. When the Danes destroyed the abbey in AD 874 these mines passed into the ownership of the Danish King Ceolwulf and thereafter became the property of the crown.

It is thought that the Cumberland, Masson and Rutland caverns at Matlock were originally lead mines.

Much of the Derbyshire lead in the 11th, 12th and 13th centuries was sent to castles and religious houses for roofing and other building purposes. In the late 12th century approximately 200 tons were exported to France.

Derbyshire's largest mine was the Mill Close mine at Darley Dale which employed some 800 miners in the 1930s. They extracted around 30,000 tons of lead annually.

Recurring explosions due to firedamp claimed many lives and the miners were in constant danger of suffering from choke damp for which the treatment was to lie face downwards on the ground breathing over freshly exposed soil from which a sod had just been removed.

Flooding was always the most serious problem in the lead mines and, in 1938, after the pumps were unable to cope with the sudden rush of water in Mill Close mine, it was shut down thus bringing to an end large scale mining in the area.

Magpie Mine at Sheldon flourished in the 18th century and was worked until flooding caused its closure. Local people believed a curse had been put on this mine, the revenge of three widows whose husbands had been killed there in 1833.

Many superstitions were held by lead miners and their families through the centuries. All the mines were thought to be inhabited by a ghost or an elf who was held responsible for any casualties or unexplained incidents occurring in or around the mines. Dreams were said to foretell deaths through accidents and it was claimed that fresh veins of lead were often discovered as a result of directions given in a dream. Whistling in a mine was frowned on as the sound was thought to drive away the ore and no miner would risk bad luck brought about by working on Good Friday.

The length of each shift in a lead mine was usually eight hours or six hours in very wet working conditions. The men wore leather clothing and a leather hat in the brim of which was fastened a candle for they all worked by candle light below ground.

Wages were based on production. In the 17th century the average pay was 5d a day for a miner and 3d for the women who washed the ore.

Lead miners were, by repute, hard workers but squandered a large proportion of their earnings. A high percentage of the men and many women smoked heavily and drank a great deal. Yet, on the whole, they were known to be 'long-livers'.

May 13th was the date on which lead miners held a Maytime celebration. After filling their 'coes', in which they kept their tools, with garlands of flowers and sprays of greenery, they sat down in the open air, if the weather permitted, to a dinner of roast beef provided either by public donations or by some Derbyshire 'notable'. Following the meal much ale was consumed as the music and singing grew louder and louder.

The rules for lead miners were passed down from generation to generation by word of mouth until 1288 when, as a result of a petition for written laws, King Edward I ordered an 'inquisition' to take place at Ashbourne with a view to establishing and setting down the rights of the miners and the principles of the industry.

The tribunal confirmed their right to 'dig and delve' in the 'King's Field' which covered most of the county with the exception of churchyards, public roads, gardens and orchards. These could not be disturbed although lead might be worked from beneath them. Any man had the privilege of seeking for lead ore without hindrance from the landowner.

In order to settle claims and disputes courts were set up in different places in the Peak District, the most notable being the Great Barmote Court at Wirksworth which survives to the present day. Twice a year, in April and October, this court meets in the Moot Hall in Chapel Lane where representations of the miners' tools are carved on the outside of the building and, inside, can be seen the great brass dish for measuring lead ore which holds 65 lbs. This was presented to the miners by King Henry VIII in 1513.

The Barmote, or Barmoot, the oldest industrial court in the world, consisted of a Steward Barmaster and 24 jurymen who undertook judicial duties continuously from the sitting of one court until the next. Called 'The Body of the Mine', these men were pledged to see that the miners received justice and this included the administration of punishments as laid down in the inquisition.

According to the ancient rules a fine was imposed for the first and second offences of stealing but, after that,

'The third time he commits such a theft
Shall have a knife stuck through his hand to the shaft
Into the stow, and there till death shall stand
Or loose himself by cutting loose his hand.'

These cruel tortures were abandoned by acts passed in 1851 to 1852 and today there are no longer any lead miners to be put on trial. But the meeting still takes place though only 12 jurymen officiate. They are traditionally provided with bread, cheese and beer and long clay pipes are distributed for smoking after the meal. If any member is absent, he is fined £5. Other courts at Hope, Eyam and Haddon meet only once during the year and follow a similar ceremony.

Apart from disused mine shafts and a few old engine houses in the Peak District, little evidence remains of the county's oldest industry, the mining of lead. Still surviving, however, are several old hostelries named 'The Jinglers' Arms' or simply 'The Jinglers' as one of the inns at Bradley is called. These recall the days when the jingle of bells on the harness could be heard of ponies making their way over the Derbyshire hills as they carried lead to all parts of the country.

Four for Revolution

IN June 1688 four noblemen arranged to meet on Whittington Moor near Chesterfield in order to devise a plan for the overthrow of King James II and to invite his nephew, the Protestant Prince William of Orange, husband of the King's daughter Mary, to be crowned King of England in his stead.

Two of the conspirators, William Cavendish, Earl of Devonshire, and Thomas Osborne, Earl of Danby, were former political enemies, Cavendish having been responsible for the latter's arrest for plotting. As a result, Osborne spent five years imprisoned in the Tower of London. They now agreed to settle their differences and together with John Darcy, grandson and heir of the Earl of Holderness, and Henry Booth, Baron Delamere, they made the journey to Whittington under the pretence of joining a hunt taking place there.

According to one account, they each contrived to draw away from it when the pack was in full cry and rode with all speed to the 'Cock and Pynot Inn'. (A pynot is the Derbyshire name for a magpie.) Another version of the story asserts that the 'Cock and Pynot' was not included in their meeting plans but, overcome by a heavy storm, they were forced to seek shelter at this old hostelry now known as 'The Revolution House'.

The Earl of Devonshire led the discussion sitting in a historic chair, on view today in Hardwick Hall, in what has been named 'The Plotting Parlour'.

Arrangements were made for Danby to organise a rising in the north of England, Devonshire undertook to raise forces in Derbyshire and the Midland counties and Delamere was to recruit an army in Cheshire. As a result of this conference, a letter was despatched to Prince William asking him to come to England with a strong army and to stand in readiness to accept the English crown. Added to their signatures were those of the Earl of Shrewsbury and the Bishop of London and the missive was sent to Holland on June 30th, carried it is said by Admiral Herbert disguised as a common sailor.

All the participants must have been aware of the great danger to their lives in undertaking such a risky enterprise.

When King James II ascended the throne on the death of his brother, King Charles II in 1685, he promised to respect the liberties of his people but before long he publicly announced his adherence to the Roman Catholic faith and began, ostentatiously, to hear Mass.

He then set about encouraging the suppression of Protestantism helped by the infamous Judge Jeffreys and his Bloody Assize which was responsible for the deaths of hundreds of people in the aftermath of Monmouth's Rebellion. This rebellion was headed by the Duke of Monmouth, one of Charles II's illegitimate sons and a claimant to the throne. It was put down and Monmouth was beheaded. But the people's indignation at the king's many broken promises and his persecution of the Covenanters continued to rise and revolts broke out all over the country with a demand for his dethronement.

A number of noblemen made their way to the Hague, taking with them large sums of money collected for the cause and Prince William of Orange prepared to raise an army. On hearing that King James's second wife, Mary of Modena, had given birth to a son who was a Stuart heir to the throne, William lost no time in setting sail for England. He anchored at Torbay on November 5th and marched at the head of 13,000 men, both English and Dutch, to Exeter. From there he was

101

soon on his way to London, hailed all the way as a deliverer.

In the meantime the forces raised by the four Whittington plotters were united under the leadership of the Earl of Devonshire who had mustered a large army in the Midlands supported by many lords and gentlemen from Derbyshire.

King James's wife and baby, James Francis Edward, known in later life as the Old Pretender, were smuggled across to the continent and James learned with dismay that his daughter, Anne, had fled from Whitehall and joined Devonshire in Nottingham.

'God help me,' he cried, 'for my own children have deserted me.'

On December 23rd James escaped abroad and on February 13th 1689 his other daughter, Mary, arrived from Holland to join her husband, Prince William and together they were proclaimed King and Queen of Great Britain and Ireland thus re-establishing Protestantism as the religion of the realm.

In 1788 there were commemorative rejoicings all over England. At Whittington church a sermon dedicated to the Earl of Devonshire was preached by the Reverend Samuel Pegge on his 84th birthday. Afterwards processions formed displaying banners which bore such slogans as 'The Protestant Religion and the Liberties of England we will Defend' and 'Revolted from Tyranny at Whittington 1688'.

As the enthusiasm of the marchers increased, many songs were sung about the Whittington Plot.

'Now Devonshire in All Saints' lies,
Although his bones are rotten,
His glorious fame will ever rise
And never be forgotten'.

On June 2nd 1988 a red helicopter landed in the grounds of the Mary Swanwick school at Old Whittington. From it stepped Prince Charles to join 2,000 people including the present Duke of Devonshire and descendants of the other plotters who were there to meet him and celebrate the Glorious Revolution which took place 300 years before.

All For Love

DESCRIBED as the most romantic medieval manor house in England, Haddon Hall stands overlooking the banks of the river Wye not far from Bakewell. Much of its appeal lies in its skilful preservation which has left it looking exactly as it would have done in the 17th century. Surrounded by meadows, its ancient walls are covered in creepers and the beautiful gardens slope down to the meandering river.

There was a dwelling on the site of Haddon Hall at the time of the Domesday Book when the manor was given to William Peverel, the illegitimate son of William the Conqueror.

After 1190 the Vernons, who had come from Normandy with the Conqueror, were in possession of the manor until 350 years later when Dorothy Vernon married into the Manners family and inherited the Hall which the Manners have held ever since. How this came about is a story of secret romance.

Sir George Vernon succeeded to the Haddon estates in 1517. Known as 'The King of the Peak', he was a formidable character and lived in an elaborate manner. He was famous for his lavish hospitality and carried out, in impressive style, many additions to the Hall. An autocrat, he was looked upon with awe and sometimes fear by both his family and his servants. He once ordered his men to hang a murderer caught in the act, without a trial. For this, he received much criticism.

After Sir George's first wife died, leaving two daughters,

Margaret and Dorothy, he began to look for a suitable bride who would supply him with an heir. His choice fell on Maud Longford, daughter of Lady Port and a descendant of Sir Anthony Fitzherbert. Maud came from the village near Ashbourne which now bears her name. Forced into the marriage by her family, she was only a few years older than her stepdaughters whom she resented. Her bridegroom was more than twice her age and came to resent her because she seemed incapable of breeding.

The story of Sir George's daughter Dorothy Vernon handed down through the years tells of her secret love affair with her cousin, John Manners, second son of the Earl of Rutland.

Because of her father's objection to the match, the lovers were said to have met clandestinely in the grounds of Haddon Hall, John being disguised as a forester. Their wooing was protected by Dorothy's maid who passed messages between them and kept a careful look-out at each assignation. On one occasion, Dorothy had barely time to slip into bed, fully dressed, before her stepmother, Dame Maud, appeared, anxious to check that Dorothy was safely indoors.

After being forbidden by her father to communicate with John, Dorothy was denied anything more than an occasional message from him for over a year and the girl's health began to decline.

It was said that Sir George would have approved a member of the Vernon family at Sudbury as a husband for Dorothy but he let it be known that any young Derbyshire man belonging to a wealthy Catholic family would be welcomed as a son-in-law.

Eventually, however, he began to make arrangements for Dorothy's betrothal to Sir Edward Stanley, son of Lord Derby and brother to her sister Margaret's husband. This news threw Dorothy into a state of panic and she was finally persuaded by John to elope.

With the help of her faithful maid, she managed to escape through the window of her bedchamber on to a terrace. Carrying only a small bundle of clothes, she ran down a flight

104

of steps to reach a footbridge over the river Wye. There John awaited her and she flew into his arms. With him were two horses for their planned journey to the family estates in Leicestershire and it is believed that they spent the first night of their elopement at Allestree, staying at the Red Cow Inn. 'There', wrote an essayist, 'on the outskirts of Derby they paused. Gold procured refreshment and two fresh horses and a sidesaddle and respectable riding habit for Dorothy. The morning mists were rising as they passed through Derby on their way to the manor of Aylestone where they married.' It was the spring of 1563.

This version of the night's events has been condemned as utterly false for neither steps nor bridge were there before the 17th century. Critics are also sceptical of the statement that Sir George Vernon had raised objections to his daughter's suitor although it was reported that he was heard referring to his prospective son-in-law as 'a nobody' and the 'beggarly son of a new earl'.

But it is possible that the disapproval of the Vernon family was on account of religious differences between the families.

An alternative story that Dorothy escaped at midnight from the ball following her sister's wedding to Sir Thomas Stanley is rejected by many people because Dorothy was five years younger than Margaret and would, at that time, have been only thirteen years of age.

The Dorothy Vernon narrative appeared in 1822 in the form of a romantic novel which was, at first, regarded as pure fiction but by many readers a contrasting view was held. They were convinced that the novelist used the true facts surrounding the elopement, merely embellishing them with the steps and the bridge. Nevertheless, the 'Dorothy Vernon steps' as they are now called, are viewed with keen interest by thousands of visitors to Haddon every year.

Dorothy and her husband were reconciled with Sir George before his death in 1567 and attended his funeral in Bakewell church where he was buried under a large altar tomb which supports the effigies of himself and his two wives. The dates of their deaths are left blank.

As there were no male heirs, the 30 manors owned by Sir George were divided between Margaret and Dorothy, the latter inheriting the Derbyshire estates including Haddon where she and her husband went to live with their family.

Sir George's widow, Maud, lost no time in marrying the man she had been forced to reject on her marriage to Sir George. He was Sir Francis Hastings, a younger brother of the Earl of Huntingdon. With this union she gave up the lands and life interest in Haddon left to her by Sir George Vernon. She died, still childless, in 1596 and, although her effigy is in Bakewell church, she was actually buried in Somerset.

Dorothy died, aged 39, in June 1594. Her husband was knighted in 1603 and eight years afterwards he also died and was buried with her in the tomb he had erected to their memory in the Vernon Chapel in Bakewell church.

Their son, George, inherited the Vernon estates and he married Grace Pierrepont who founded the Lady Manners School in Bakewell. Their grandson, John, succeeded his cousin as 8th Earl of Rutland and Haddon, today, is still owned by the Dukes of Rutland, descendants of Dorothy Vernon.

Pack Rag Day

'Good morning, Mister Martinmas,
You've come to set me free
For I don't care for master
And he don't care for me.
I'm going to the Mop Fair,
Today's the day I'm free'.

MARTINMAS, November 11th, was a popular time for hiring fairs to be held and they often lasted three days 'on vigil, feast and morrow'. After the Black Death there was a shortage of agricultural labourers and a law was passed directing all able-bodied men to offer themselves for hire. Farm hands were engaged for fifty-one weeks because a person who became unemployed after less than one full year's work was not eligible for Parish Relief.

This was an occasion for those who had been engaged at the last hiring fair, had been found unsatisfactory and given notice, to find new masters. Others, dissatisfied with their working conditions, waited for Pack Rag Day, hoping to be offered a better situation at the Runaway Mop Fair. This tale tells of a typical farmer's day out at the hiring fair at Chapel-en-le-Frith in the last century.

The farmer's wife emerged from the fowl cote holding two

107

squawking hens, their legs tied together. She threw them into the back of the cart as her husband backed the horse between the shafts and a boy, bleary eyed, stumbled out of the kitchen door. After swilling his face under the pump, he climbed on to the cart wheel and jumped inside to join the hens.

'Look sharp, lass', called his mother hurrying across the yard and, as she entered the farmhouse, a buxom dark eyed girl with a bundle under her arm and a mop in her hand, pushed past her and clambered into the cart. The farmer pulled himself up in front and shook the reins.

'Bring some fairings for t'bairns,' shouted his wife as the cart jolted out of the farmyard, then added, putting her hands round her mouth, 'and mind what sort o' wench thou brings this time and good shuts to that 'un.' The girl in the cart turned and put her thumb to her nose.

An early morning mist enveloped the hills as they splashed through the ford, bumped along a stony track for half a mile and came out on to the turnpike road from Glossop where the going was easier. Here they joined other carts and wagons and many country folk on foot, some with baskets of dairy produce on their arms, some driving sheep or cattle with the help of dogs and many curses.

Once, a gentleman on horseback, his groom riding behind, galloped through the throng, scattering animals and men and causing more than one cart to overturn into the ditch.

As the sun lifted itself from behind Kinder Scout and penetrated the mist in the valley, the farmer gazed across the pattern of dry stone walls to the purple hills in the distance.

'Look', he cried, pointing with his whip and, among the sheep grazing on the slopes could be seen a Kinder hare, its coat now almost white in readiness for the winter.

Soon the woods were alive with birdsong, cocks were crowing and, as they passed through Hayfield, smoke climbed straight up from cottage chimneys. Appearing from nowhere, beggars began to line the roadsides, stretching out their hands as the cavalcade went by.

'Why is Tilly going to leave us?' the boy asked his father as he stood up to wait for a glimpse of the Kinder Downfall which came into view from time to time, its clouds of spray sparkling in the sunlight. ' 'Twas only at Michaelmas you brought her from the fair at Tideswell.'

'She be too comely,' his father replied. 'Yer mother knew no peace with 'er in t'ouse.'

Tilly tossed her head as he turned to give her a wink.

'Pack Rag day gives servants a chance to make a change, an' all', was her retort.

Progressing more slowly now on the uphill road to Chapel-en-le-Frith, they passed the Lamb Inn, the house called the Peep o'Day and came, before long, to the outskirts of the town.

Leaving the horse in Carrier's Meadow, tethered to a tree, the three of them threaded their way through the town's narrow streets, following a scissor grinder with his barrow, until they came to the cobbled market place where, already, a couple of pickpockets were sitting with their feet in the stocks. Past stalls selling candles and firewood, caged birds and rabbits, they soon found a poulterer where the two hens changed hands for ninepence apiece. On the steps of the ancient market cross stood a group of servants waiting to be hired.

Here, where a man once took his wife, a halter round her neck, to be sold to the highest bidder, shepherds held their crooks, dairymaids clasped milking stools and carters carried whips to indicate their calling.

'Be off with you', said the farmer to Tilly, giving her a parting slap on the buttocks, and she joined the female servants holding mops.

Employers seeking a farm hand examined the men as if they were beasts, feeling their arm muscles, spanning the breadth of their shoulders and sometimes opening their mouths to scrutinize their teeth. Deals were struck by placing a coin in the servant's palm. The employer would spit on it and the servant would then slap his hand down on it to seal the bargain.

A generous employer might then take his new farm man for a drink.

The boy surveyed the housemaids with mops and thought what a poor assortment they were, apart from Tilly, and was not surprised to see, within a few minutes, a florid faced man present her with a fasten coin. Thus, officially hired, she was free to enjoy the attractions of the fair until she was taken home by her new employer.

'Tha's tekkin on a load o' trouble for thy missus,' the farmer warned the man as Tilly slipped away among the stalls but the man replied, 'My missus be dead. The lass will serve two purposes'.

Now the boy and his father made their way to the cattle pens where trade was brisk and farmers counted their animals by means of Derbyshire shepherds' numbers:

'Ain tain tethera fethera fimp
sethera lethera hovera dovera dick
aindick taindick tetherdick fetherdick bumfy
ainbumfy tainbumfy tetherbumfy fetherbumfy kicky'.

Returning to the market cross, they found the same pitiful group still leaning on their mops and the boy watched uneasily as his father ordered them, one by one, to extend their arms in order to demonstrate their 'reach'. Several of them were old and bent and looked incapable of doing a day's work. There were two open mouthed slatterns whom the farmer judged to be half-wits and a pale, thin child who answered his question, 'How old arta?' in a frightened whisper, 'Near fourteen, maister'. At least his wife would have no misgivings about this one, he reflected and slapped a penny in her hand.

'Be at t'cattle pens at sunset', he bade her then led his son to the part of the fair where cheapjacks were selling their wares from the backs of carts. They examined knives, buckles, belts and harness and the farmer bought gew-gaws for the children and laces for their mother. Sauntering round the fairground, they paused at the booth where quack doctors sold nostrums for every ailment and the toothpuller's assistant promised a reduction for extracting two teeth at once, banging his drum to drown the screams of the victims.

At noon, the farmer put a nosebag on his horse and, after buying oatcakes and a pippin pasty for the boy, he pushed his way through the crowds to the ale tent. The boy wandered round the peepshows, inspecting a fat lady and a two-headed goat and spent a pleasant hour watching cock fighting and bear baiting. He joined in pelting with rotten fruit a man fastened in the pillory for giving short weight and watched several sparring matches between two gangs of youths.

The smell from rotting vegetables and putrid fish grew stronger as the day wore on and a wagon load of animal skins gave off a nauseous stench. As the sun went down, stallholders shouted reductions in the prices of their goods, offering to accept rabbit skins in payment instead of money.

The boy now found his way back to the almost empty cattle pens where the frail little girl stood patiently waiting. Before long, the farmer turned up in a jocular mood, having done the round of the town's taverns.

From the fairground came the sound of fiddles being tuned up and, suddenly Tilly appeared running towards them. Flinging her arms round the farmer's neck, she planted a hot kiss on his mouth. 'Farewell, maister', she said then lifted up her skirts and skipped off to join the dancers.

'Shameless hussy', he said, wiping his hand across his mouth, but there was a look of longing in his eyes as they followed her across the field.

They untethered the horse and, as the first stars appeared, set off on the journey home while the strains of 'Come lasses and lads', the original Peak District Fair song, came over the evening air. On the skyline a rotting body on a gibbet swung to and fro. The girl shivered and yawned then slid down on to the straw at the bottom of the cart and shortly fell asleep. Exhausted humans and animals plodded along the road, kept awake by an occasional drunken brawl but mainly by singing, in a variety of keys, the county's most popular song, 'The Derby Ram'.

'As I was going to market, sir, upon a market day,
I met the finest ram, sir,
That ever was fed on hay.

This ram was fat behind sir,
This ram was fat before,
This ram was ten yards high, sir,
Indeed he could've been more.

The wool upon his back, sir,
Reached up into the sky,
The eagles built their nests there,
I heard the young ones cry.

The man that fed the ram, sir,
He fed him twice a day,
And every time they fed him, sir,
He ate a rick of hay.

The devil once rode this ram, sir,
The Derby folk do tell,
But the ram just hunched his back, sir,
And sent him straight to hell.'

At Hayfield the River Sett shone silver in the moonlight and they rumbled over the bridge, recently damaged by floods that had swept away corpses from the churchyard.

Seeing that the boy was also asleep, the farmer turned into the market place, pulling up outside the Packhorse Inn, and went inside. Much later, he emerged and climbed unsteadily into the cart. The horse, familiar with the road, jogged wearily home.

As they turned into the farmyard, the boy awoke and helped

his father to unharness the horse while, across the yard, came his mother, a lantern in her hand. Holding it aloft, she peered into the cart and uttered a cry.

'What's to do, woman?' Her husband's voice was thick and slurred.

She stared in dismay at the girl's emaciated limbs, her transparent skin and the dusky eyelashes lying on unhealthily flushed cheeks.

'God's death, man', she whispered hoarsely. 'Thou's brought one trouble in exchange for another. We're rid o' the strumpet but this child will soon need a shroud.'

A
Mock Marriage

AN unmarried clergyman, the Rev Joseph Hunt, was appointed to the living of Eyam, the Plague village, on March 21st 1684. For some time he had been engaged to a young lady of Derby, said to be 'of some social status', and it was assumed that, as soon as he was settled among his new parishioners in Eyam, their wedding would take place and his bride would live with him there.

Not long after the rector took up his new post he was asked to baptise a child belonging to Matthew Ferns, the landlord of an inn in the village called 'The Miners' Arms'. The ceremony over, Mr. Hunt was pressed to join in the celebrations which followed and these included a great deal of drinking. Becoming more than a little inebriated, he began to make advances to the landlord's eighteen year old daughter, Anne. Encouraged by others in the party who were also 'under the influence', the young rector agreed to go through a mock marriage ceremony with Anne, using the Book of Common Prayer and each making the customary vows while one of the party acted as minister.

Scandalised when they heard of this episode, a number of people in the village lost no time in supplying the Bishop of the Diocese with details of the affair. The bishop ruled that Mr. Hunt should marry Miss Ferns as soon as possible in the proper manner so that the union could be legally confirmed. The marriage was then consecrated in church on September 4th 1684 but, unfortunately, his ex-fiancee in Derby sued him for breach of promise.

The litigation expenses incurred reduced him to poverty and, in order to avoid being arrested, he moved with his wife into the church vestry. This building was enlarged for their convenience and the couple made it their home for the rest of their lives, both their children being born there.

In addition to carrying out his ecclesiastical duties in the parish, Mr. Hunt spent many hours in rewriting the church registers, dating from 1630 to 1705. These include the lists of 260 victims who died from the Plague in 1665 and 1666.

The Rev Joseph Hunt died in December 1709. His wife had died six years previously and both lie buried in the vestry which had been their home for the whole of their married life.

The Pretender
Comes to Derby

'God bless the King – I mean our faith's defender.
God bless (no harm in blessing) the Pretender,
But who Pretender is and who the King,
God bless us all, that's quite another thing.'

DUSK had fallen on the evening of December 4th 1745 when HRH Prince Charles Edward Stuart arrived in the county town of Derby. Known as Bonnie Prince Charlie, he was almost twenty-five and described as 'a fine person, 6 feet high and with a majestic presence'. He wore tartan dress and a white wig which was covered by a Scottish bonnet adorned with a white rose.

Attended by a bodyguard of Scottish lords and the music of bagpipes, the Prince rode down Friargate and into the market place where he received an enthusiastic welcome. His father, the Old Pretender, was proclaimed by the Town Crier as King James the Third and, to the accompaniment of peals of church bells, the Young Pretender was escorted to Exeter House in Full Street.

When the citizens of Derby heard that Prince Charles was shortly expected in the town at the head of a large army, many residents gathered up their valuables and fled to neighbouring villages for they believed the tales that the 'hairy men from the Highlands' were rapists, eating babies and boiling their captives alive in whisky!

On the night of December 3rd the Duke of Devonshire held a meeting in Derby at the George Inn, Irongate, where it was decided that he and the twelve companies of soldiers, all raised by subscription 'to support the Royal Person and Government of His Majesty King George the Second against the Popish Pretender' should withdraw by torchlight to Nottingham, which they did. This was in order to spare the men's lives as the Duke had received information that the Pretender's army was so large that he had no hope of bringing about its defeat.

The Prince, gratified by the loyal support he received in the Highlands after landing in Scotland in August, marched steadily southwards, hoping to pick up more troops on the way. Having crossed the border with no more than a few skirmishes, he occupied Carlisle and then Lancaster and Preston but failed to get many adherents for his planned march to London where he intended to claim the English throne on behalf of his father, now living abroad in retirement.

During his advance through the Midlands he was warned to expect a frosty reception in Derby for a circular from the Privy Council, sent to the Justices of the town, directed that 'any unlawful riots, assemblies or tumults that might accompany the Prince's visit' should be immediately suppressed.

The Jacobite rebels reached Leek in Staffordshire on December 3rd and, early the following morning, were on their way to Ashbourne where the Prince had spent the night with Major General Sir William Boothby, Bt., at Ashbourne Hall, former seat of the Cokayne family. The Prince was proclaimed at the market cross before setting out for Derby. Mr Meynell at Bradley Hall took the precaution of burying his silver in the garden before preparing to meet the Prince and his followers who pressed on through Mugginton, Weston Underwood and Kedleston.

A warning that troops occupied the surrounding hills caused

the army to be on the alert for battle but the 'enemy soldiers' turned out to be a crowd of local gentry and their retainers, eager to catch a glimpse of His Royal Highness.

Breaking his journey in order to lunch at Radbourne Hall with Colonel Pole, a Tory squire, the Prince was disappointed that the sum of money he had expected to receive from his host, contributed by his supporters in the Midlands, did not materialise. These funds had, in fact, been collected but had mysteriously disappeared.

The afternoon of December 4th saw the arrival of two Jacobite officers in Derby. They demanded billets for 900 men and were soon joined by 30 Hussars who requisitioned horses, arms and public money. Three hours later, the Life Guards appeared, said to be 'in fine fettle' but mounted on 'poor jaded horses'.

Thereafter, a motley assembly of foot soldiers straggled into the town. A mixture of every rank, 'from childhood to old age, from the dwarf to the giant, many walking barefoot with dirty shirts and without breeches', these dejected followers evoked pity rather than fear in the hearts of the onlookers.

Officers found accommodation with such prominent people as Mr. Thomas Gisborne at his residence in the Wardwick, now called Jacobean House, Mr. Franceys, the famous apothecary, Mr. Heathcote whose house stood in the market place and Mr. Samuel Crompton at Friary House, now the Friary Hotel.

Ordinary citizens had the hungry, lice-ridden foot sloggers billeted upon them, depleting their larders and consuming quantities of ale. One householder said they 'stank and looked like fiends out of hell'. Number 28, Irongate, the house where Joseph Wright, the artist, was born, was taken over by 43 soldiers, the Wright family having hastily departed to Repton for safety.

Meanwhile, Prince Charles and his chief attendants dined at Exeter House whose owner, Lord Exeter, together with the Mayor, Robert Hague, and the Town Clerk, William Bateman, had hastily left before they arrived. It is believed that, because

119

the Mayor's conscience smote him for deserting his municipality on such an occasion, he returned to Derby and went straight to Exeter House with the intention of paying his respects to the Prince. Unfortunately, however, he asked for an audience with 'the Pretender' whereupon the Scottish guard kicked him down the stairs, shouting that the Pretender could be found occupying the throne of England.

The Prince and his principal officers discussed plans for his journey south and his entry into London. They heard with satisfaction that the advance guard was now in possession of Swarkestone Bridge, a few miles south of Derby, and the Prince retired to bed full of optimism for a successful military operation.

On the morning of the 5th an air of excitement pervaded the town and everyone was early astir. The refreshed troops now ran amok, stealing goods from the shops and even taking gloves, buckles, kerchiefs and anything they fancied from the people wearing them. Letters despatched by the Prince's soldiers in Derby all expressed enthusiasm for the enterprise and eagerness for the continued march south.

Prince Charles attended a Roman Catholic mass in All Saints' church and afterwards there were more debates but these developed into a stormy Council of War regarding the army's future prospects. The Prince was confounded by Lord George Murray's advice that they should immediately retreat, declaring that their numbers were too small for such an undertaking and, even if they reached London, they would find it impossible to capture the capital in the face of Government troops. He pointed out that there had been little success in obtaining contributions to the Prince's funds in Derbyshire and recruitment had been a dismal failure notwithstanding the gift of five shillings made to each man signing on and a promise of five guineas on reaching London. Only three Derby men had volunteered for the Prince's army, – Edward Hewitt, a butcher, a blacksmith named Cooke and James Sparks, a stocking maker. In addition, news was brought that a force of 8,000 soldiers was stationed at Lichfield ready to intercept the Prince's army on the way to London.

Prince Charles was furious, accusing his officers of betrayal but, with extreme reluctance, he agreed to retreat and abandon 'this irresponsible enterprise'. Extra soldiers were sent to guard the bridge at Swarkestone while the withdrawal got underway. Angry and disillusioned at the change of plans, the troops rampaged through the town, looting food and clothing. Early next morning, leaving filth and lice behind them, they moved off sullenly en route for Ashbourne. Here they commandeered horses, carts and produce for use on their long journey back north, many Highlanders deserting on the way.

The Young Pretender and the last of his followers having departed, there was a great rejoicing in Derby. The town dignitaries soon returned and joined a large crowd of citizens in front of the Guildhall where they publicly drank a toast to King George II.

In the following April the Jacobite army was massacred at Culloden Moor, near Inverness and Prince Charles escaped to the Island of Skye with the help of Flora Macdonald. From there he sailed for France and ended his life, a 'drunken and disappointed man', living in perpetual exile.

The Amazing
Flying Donkey

YOUNG people in Derby were always eager to take up some new pastime and, if this contained an element of danger, it was all the more exciting.

Two hundred and sixty years ago a Frenchman called Gillinoe undertook to entertain the townspeople by carrying out a series of perilous exploits on a rope. This was stretched from the top of All Saints' church, now the cathedral, to the tower of Saint Michael's church, some fifty yards away.

Balancing himself on a breastplate, conveniently grooved to prevent slipping, Monsieur Gillinoe slid down the rope. During transit which lasted about eight seconds, he blew a trumpet and fired a pistol. Each day he made the descent twice over and a spectator at one of these performances reported that it quickly caught the imagination of the audience which increased in number daily.

During the next two years the 'Flying Rage', as it was called, continued to fascinate the young people of Derby and the surrounding neighbourhood. Walls, posts, trees, houses and all kinds of buildings were climbed for the thrill of flying down from them. Dogs and cats, terrified no doubt, were made to slide down ropes from great heights. Rope races were held and bets were taken for the fastest speed without a fall. 'No amusement,' observed a contemporary writer, 'could compare with the rope.'

A boy named Cadman became a popular performer. He slid down a rope from All Saints' tower in different positions. With a piece of grooved wood fastened to his back and one to his chest, he made the descent face downwards, on his back with arms and legs outstretched, sitting erect or, occasionally, standing with one foot on the rope while he waved to the crowds below. Sometimes the velocity of his flight created fire by friction and he was followed by a stream of smoke which raised cheers from the onlookers.

The diversion was finally brought to an end in 1734 when a disreputable individual arrived in Derby with a donkey and volunteered to surpass all former displays of flying. He stretched a rope from All Saints' tower to the bottom of St. Mary's Gate where it was securely fastened. His programme began by sliding down the rope, drawing after him a wheelbarrow in which sat a thirteen year old boy. This feat he repeated several times and proposed to follow it by a similar flight on the rope by his donkey.

The first part of the stunt was accomplished successfully, man, boy and wheelbarrow having landed safely. 'Then,' wrote an eye witness, 'the vast multitude turned their eyes towards the ass.' The poor animal had been taken up to the tower the previous day and had been heard, constantly braying, either from fear or want of food. Now, with half a hundredweight of lead attached to each of its feet, it was manoeuvred astride the rope and began its descent.

Excitement grew as the donkey sped downwards and the spectators maintained a breathless silence. Suddenly, about twenty yards from the County Hall, the rope broke. The donkey was precipitated, head first, into the crowd and all was noise and confusion. Shrieks and shouts came from the frightened onlookers thrown to the ground but, surprisingly, the donkey was not hurt. Its fall had been cushioned by the mass of bodies on which it landed.

No lives were lost but, at the other end of the street, a number of people were injured by falling masonry where the breaking of the rope had brought down a chimney.

This catastrophe put an end to the craze for flying and the instigator of the latest feat who had expected to collect generous donations in appreciation, sneaked ignominiously out of Derby with his long suffering donkey.